FALSECARDS

by Mike Lawrence

**Published by
Devyn Press, Inc.
Louisville, Kentucky**

Conver by Bonnie Baron Pollack

Printed in the United States of America.

Devyn Press, Inc.
151 Thierman Lane
Louisville, KY 40207

ISBN 0-910791-47-3

CONTENTS

Introduction

FALSECARDS IN GENERAL

Before getting into specific hands and circumstances, I would like to offer a bit of advice relating to falsecards.

DON'T BOTHER WITH THEM!

If this seems like peculiar advice to find in a book on falsecards, well, it is. In general, defense is the hardest part of bridge. It is difficult enough when you know what is going on. It's nearly impossible when you have to guess. If you insist on sending out a bewildering array of signals, you will nail an occasional declarer or two. But you will also nail your partner.

Bridge is a partnership game. One or two or three successes will not compensate for a confused, embarrassed, or upset partner.

Ever had this experience?

```
              ♠ K J 3 2
              ♡ K J 4 3
              ◊ Q 5
              ♣ Q 8 2
♠ A 9 8
♡ Q 8 2        N
◊ J 6 3      W   E
♣ A K J 5      S
```

North	South
	1 ◊
1 ♡	1 ♠
3 ♠ (1)	4 ♠
Pass	

(1) Invitational

You lead the ♣K and partner plays the three. There's is no way you are going to beat this on high cards, but there may be a way to promote a trump trick. Three things must happen.

1. Clubs must be 4-3-3-3
2. Partner must have the ♠10
3. Declarer must lead a spade from dummy to his queen.

If all this happens, you will win the first round of spades, and lead the thirteenth club. This will promote a trump trick.

All this happening is against the odds, but something is better than nothing.

Putting it into practice, you continue with the ♠A and another club. They turn out to be 4-3-3-3. Declarer wins and leads the ♠2 to his queen and your ace.

The good news is that partner has the ♠10. The bad news is that he has just played it.

When you lead the ♣J (partner might have the ♠7), declarer guesses the position and makes the rest.

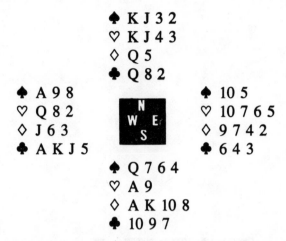

♠ K J 3 2
♥ K J 4 3
♦ Q 5
♣ Q 8 2

♠ A 9 8
♥ Q 8 2
♦ J 6 3
♣ A K J 5

♠ 10 5
♥ 10 7 6 5
♦ 9 7 4 2
♣ 6 4 3

♠ Q 7 6 4
♥ A 9
♦ A K 10 8
♣ 10 9 7

What went wrong? On declarer's chosen line of play, 4♠ was going down. Why did partner ruin your plans?

The answer is that partner was falsecarding. He thought declarer might have the ♠A. Partner played the ten, hoping to discourage declarer from finessing in spades if the situation were as below.

♠ K J 3 2

♠ Q 9 8   ♠ 10 5

♠ A 7 6 4

This was the layout partner was hoping for.

Partner was trying to do a good thing. It just happened that on this occasion, it cost a game contract.

You may form your own conclusion.

PART I

FALSECARDS BY THE DEFENDERS

Chapter 1

FALSECARDS BY THE OPENING LEADER

There are a number of valid reasons for choosing to lead an unusual card. These reasons include:

1. You might lead third or fifth best in order to mislead declarer as to your length in the suit. (This assumes you normally lead fourth best.)
2. You might lead the "wrong" card from a sequence in order to mislead declarer as to where the high cards are, i.e., lead the jack from QJx.
3. You might underlead an ace against a suit contract.

Note that you *do not* make an unusual lead simply because you feel like it. You do it because there is a specific, defined, reason for it. Falsecards are dangerous because they mislead partner as well as declarer. If you falsecard ten times and get five good results, four normal results, and embarrass partner once, you can be sure partner will remember the tenth time. He won't like it, and worse, it may cause him to doubt your carding in the future.

Leading Fifth Best or Third Best

Both vulnerable — North deals.

West
- ♠ Q 8 2
- ♡ 9 2
- ◊ A 8 6
- ♣ A Q 8 6 2

West	North	East	South
	1♠	Pass	2◊
Pass	2♠	Pass	3 NT
Pass	Pass	Pass	

With a perfectly good club holding, it is right to lead one. Normally, you would lead the six, and unless you can find reason to do otherwise, you should do so.

In this instance, you can anticipate that the spade suit will run. If declarer chooses to play on spades, you know that he will succeed.

But! If declarer doesn't fear the club suit, he may decide to knock out your ◊ A.

The entire hand might look like this.

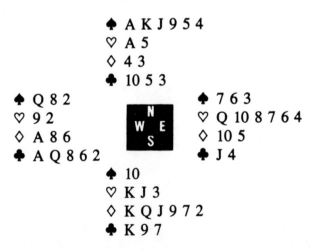

	♠ A K J 9 5 4	
	♡ A 5	
	◊ 4 3	
	♣ 10 5 3	

♠ Q 8 2		♠ 7 6 3
♡ 9 2		♡ Q 10 8 7 6 4
◊ A 8 6		◊ 10 5
♣ A Q 8 6 2		♣ J 4

	♠ 10	
	♡ K J 3	
	◊ K Q J 9 7 2	
	♣ K 9 7	

If declarer thinks clubs are 5-2, he can't afford to lead diamonds. He will try for spades, and those will work.

If declarer thinks clubs are 4-3, he will play on diamonds expecting to lose three clubs and one diamond.

If you lead the ♣2 on this hand, declarer would expect clubs to be non-dangerous and would try the diamonds.

Conversely,

Both vulnerable

> *West*
> ♠ 8 7 3
> ♡ 9 4 2
> ◇ A 8 6
> ♣ A Q 6 2

West	*North*	*East*	*South*
	1 ♠	Pass	2 ◇
Pass	2 ♣	Pass	3 NT
Pass	Pass	Pass	

You could, in theory, lead the ♣6. If declarer can be talked into believing you have five of them, he may try the spade finesse rather than knock out the ◇A.

Analysis of Leading Third or Fifth Best

These falsecards are unlikely to occur. The situation has to be just right and you run the risk that partner will do the wrong thing.

The necessary conditions are

1. You must have nearly all the critical cards held by the defenders so that partner will not be taking an active part in the defense.
2. You must be able to clearly predict how the play of the hand will go and what effect your falsecard will have.

11

Leading fifth best may occur once a year, leading third best even less.

Underleading an Ace vs. a Suit Contract

Considering the number of times this lead is attempted, one might believe it were more the rule than the exception.
Some of the time it works. And some of the time it doesn't. There are two problems with underleading aces:

1. There is frequently a better alternative, including leading the ace instead of underleading it.
2. Even when it's right, it's wrong.

For instance.

No one vulnerable — West deals

```
                  ♠ Q 6 2
                  ♡ J 8 3
                  ◇ Q 5
                  ♣ Q 10 6 4 2
    ♠ 8                          ♠ A 5 3
    ♡ A 5 2          N           ♡ K 10 9 6 4
    ◇ J 8 7 6 2   W     E        ◇ A 9 4
    ♣ J 9 8 5         S          ♣ 7 3
                  ♠ K J 10 9 7 4
                  ♡ Q 7
                  ◇ K 10 3
                  ♣ A K
```

West	North	East	South
Pass	Pass	1 ♡	1 ♠
2 ♡	2 ♠	Pass	4 ♠
Pass	Pass	Pass	

This auction wasn't too accurate, but it could happen. And, if the defense goofs, 4♠ can make.

How can the defense goof? Easy. If West leads the ♡2, East has to guess whether the lead is from Axx, in which case, he has to play the king, or whether the lead is from Qxx, in which case the nine is correct. In this case, the king would be necessary.

Or,

North - South vulnerable — North deals.

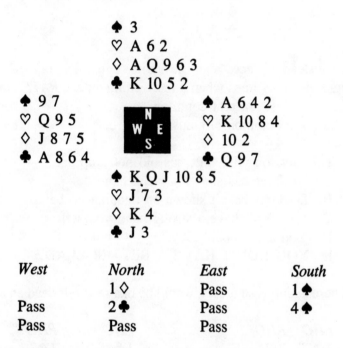

```
              ♠ 3
              ♡ A 6 2
              ◊ A Q 9 6 3
              ♣ K 10 5 2
♠ 9 7                        ♠ A 6 4 2
♡ Q 9 5          N           ♡ K 10 8 4
◊ J 8 7 5      W   E         ◊ 10 2
♣ A 8 6 4        S           ♣ Q 9 7
              ♠ K Q J 10 8 5
              ♡ J 7 3
              ◊ K 4
              ♣ J 3
```

West	North	East	South
	1◊	Pass	1♠
Pass	2♣	Pass	4♠
Pass	Pass	Pass	

If West leads a heart, the contract goes down routinely. If West leads a cagey little club, the contract will succeed if East plays the ♣9 instead of the queen.

East should play the queen, you say? Perhaps. But if the hand is as follows, the queen will be a disaster.

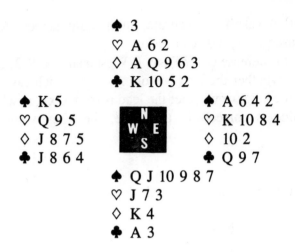

```
              ♠ 3
              ♡ A 6 2
              ◇ A Q 9 6 3
              ♣ K 10 5 2
♠ K 5                        ♠ A 6 4 2
♡ Q 9 5         N            ♡ K 10 8 4
◇ J 8 7 5     W   E          ◇ 10 2
♣ J 8 6 4       S            ♣ Q 9 7
              ♠ Q J 10 9 8 7
              ♡ J 7 3
              ◇ K 4
              ♣ A 3
```

Underleading aces can be quite dynamic, but it's so dangerous. The times when underleading an ace *RATES* to be correct are just not that common.

The three common circumstances are:

1. Dummy, on your left, has bid notrump and:
    A. Declarer has shown a weak hand
    B. Declarer hasn't shown an unbalanced hand
    C. You don't have a strong hand yourself
    D. You are probably leading an unbid suit
    E. YOU DON'T HAVE A BETTER LEAD.

These auctions suggest it would be okay to underlead an ace.

LHO	RHO
1 NT	2♡
Pass	

LHO	RHO
1♣	1♠
1 NT	2♠

This auction is not as clear-cut.

LHO	RHO
1♣	1♠
1 NT	2♡
Pass	

With RHO showing two suits, you should think twice about underleading the ◇A.

♠ A 4 2
♡ Q 5
◇ J 9 3
♣ Q 10 7 4 2

LHO	RHO
1♣	1♡
1 NT	2♡

The ♠2 is okay because of the auction and also because nothing else stands out. You should rarely feel that underleading an ace is a wonderful thing to do.

♠ J 7 2
♡ A 4 2
◇ J 10 9 3
♣ K 5 4

LHO	RHO
1 NT	2♠

The ◇J stands out. It's very rare that you would underlead an ace when you have a solid alternative.

2. The second common situation where you can underlead an ace is on one of these sequences when:

A. You have opened the bidding
B. LHO has doubled or overcalled 1 NT
C. Your partner has bid a new suit.

YOU

West	North	East	South
1♣	Double	1♡	1♠

You might underlead the ♡A.

West	North	East	South
1♣	1 NT	2◇	2♡

You might underlead the ◇A.

15

On these sequences, LHO has implied some length and strength in the suit your partner has bid.

♠ A 3
♡ Q J 6 2
◊ K 8 5 4 2
♣ K 5

West	North	East	South
1 ◊	Double	1 ♠	2 ♡
Pass	Pass	Pass	

The ♠3 could work here. Note that nothing else stands out. Underleading an ace is a last resort.

Similarly:

♠ A J 4
♡ K 10 8 6 3
◊ A 5 3
♣ 10 3

West	North	East	South
1 ♡	1 NT	2 ◊	3 ♣
Pass	Pass	Pass	

The ◊ 3 is pretty clear cut here. An entirely possible hand is this one.

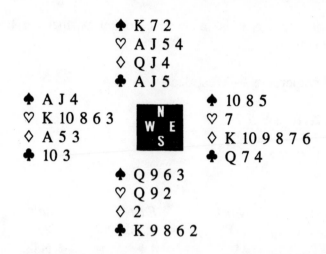

Compare how the defense goes if you start the defense with any lead other than a small diamond to partner's king.

Analysis of Underleading Aces in Either of the Above Situations

When properly done, underleading an ace can be extremely effective. In terms of frequency, I would say the occasion arises one time in twenty-five sessions. Hardly overwhelming.

One more point. If you clearly identify the proper time for this play and if partner does also, then you won't have to worry that either:

1.   Partner underled at the wrong time   or
2.   Partner will do the wrong thing when you underlead.

Note that this entire discussion has centered around the opening lead only. Later in the hand, different considerations apply.

3.   The third "frequent" situation where you might underlead an ace is not really intended to fool declarer. Rather, you

do it because it is imperative to get partner on lead immediately.

No one vulnerable — West deals

♠ A 10 8 6 5 2
♡ 7 5 3
◊ K 7 6 2
♣ —

West	North	East	South
Pass	1♣	Pass	1♡
1♠	4♡	4♠	4 NT
5♠	6◊ (1)	Pass	6♡
Pass	Pass	Pass	

(1) Three aces

Lead the ♠2. There is an excellent chance your partner has the ♠K. If so, he will work out that you underled the ♠A for a reason. He should figure it out.

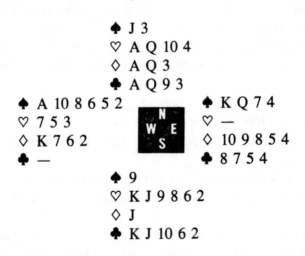

♠ J 3
♡ A Q 10 4
◊ A Q 3
♣ A Q 9 3

♠ A 10 8 6 5 2   ♠ K Q 7 4
♡ 7 5 3   ♡ —
◊ K 7 6 2   ◊ 10 9 8 5 4
♣ —   ♣ 8 7 5 4

♠ 9
♡ K J 9 8 6 2
◊ J
♣ K J 10 6 2

Not vulnerable vs. vulnerable — North deals

♠ 4 2
♡ A Q 7 3
◇ A Q 6 2
♣ 8 5 4

West	North	East	South
	1♣	2♡	2♠
4♡	Pass	Pass	4 NT
Pass	5◇	Pass	5♠
Pass	Pass	Pass	

Try the ♡3 or ♡7. Declarer should have the ◇K for his bidding. If partner has the ♡K, a diamond return will defeat 5♠.

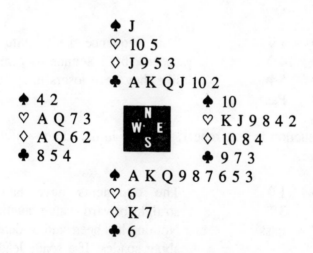

```
                 ♠ J
                 ♡ 10 5
                 ◇ J 9 5 3
                 ♣ A K Q J 10 2
  ♠ 4 2                        ♠ 10
  ♡ A Q 7 3        N           ♡ K J 9 8 4 2
  ◇ A Q 6 2     W·   E         ◇ 10 8 4
  ♣ 8 5 4          S           ♣ 9 7 3
                 ♠ A K Q 9 8 7 6 5 3
                 ♡ 6
                 ◇ K 7
                 ♣ 6
```

Analysis of Underleading an Ace
When You Require Something of Partner

This circumstance is rare, but when it comes up, it has a high likelihood of success.

Remember these guidelines:

1. You need partner to make a specific return and
2. The setting tricks won't wait.

Usually when you try this maneuver, partner has raised your suit, but in a pinch, you might try it in an unbid suit.

The rarest of all cases for underleading an ace is when the opponents have had a strong auction which SPECIFICALLY PINPOINTED a weakness. Usually, for this criteria to apply, the opponents will have climbed to the five-level.

Auctions like these are typical.

1♣	2♡	The 5♡ bid asks about spades
3♡	4♣	and the pass denies spade con-
4♢	4♡	trol.
5♡	Pass	

1♣	1♡	This sequence isn't quite as
3♡	4♢	specific but it sounds very much
4♡	5♣	like they have losers in spades.
5♡	Pass	

This auction is not, repeat, IS NOT in the same family as the above.

1♣	1♢	The opponents have had a
1♡	3♡	straightforward value auction.
4♡	Pass	Nothing has been said or denied
		about spades. If a spade lead is
		correct, and it likely is, it is more
		or less an accident.

```
♠ A J 3          LHO      RHO
♡ 8 6 4                   1♡
♦ Q J 9 7 5      2♣       3♡
♣ 10 2           4♦       4♡
                 5♡       Pass
```

The 5♡ bid asked about spades and the pass showed no spade control. Not at all unreasonable to lead the ♠3.

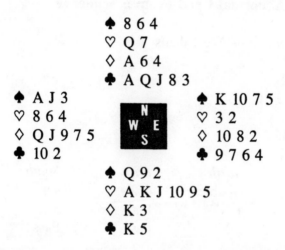

```
              ♠ 8 6 4
              ♡ Q 7
              ◊ A 6 4
              ♣ A Q J 8 3
♠ A J 3                      ♠ K 10 7 5
♡ 8 6 4                      ♡ 3 2
◊ Q J 9 7 5                  ◊ 10 8 2
♣ 10 2                       ♣ 9 7 6 4
              ♠ Q 9 2
              ♡ A K J 10 9 5
              ◊ K 3
              ♣ K 5
```

Thirteen tricks without a spade lead. Eleven tricks with the ♠A lead. And down one with the ♠3 lead. Against a strong sequence, you may not feel like underleading an ace. But, given the actual auction, it is not just reasonable, it is almost called for. Note that if the opening leader had longer spades, it would still be right to underlead the ace.

```
              9 5 4
A 8 6 2                    K J 10
              Q 7 3
```

If partner has the KJ10, you can get three tricks whether the queen is in the dummy or in declarer's hand.

```
              J 10 3
  A 8 6 5 2              K 4
              Q 9 7
```

You might even get a ruff, which was not available if you led the ace. Note that when the auction *tells* you to lead a suit, you should even underlead the AQxx(x).

Leading an Abnormal Card From a Sequence

No one vulnerable — West deals

♠ 8 6 2
♡ K Q J 10 8 6 2
◇ —
♣ J 7 3

West	North	East	South
3 ♡	Double	4 ♡	4 ♠
Pass	4 NT	Pass	5 ◇
Pass	6 ♠	Pass	Pass
Pass			

What you want to happen is to have partner win something and give you a diamond ruff. With partner raising hearts, this looks like the suit to lead. The trick is to lead a heart such that if partner wins it, he will return a diamond.

The first thing to avoid, therefore, is leading the ♡K. Partner might just let you win the trick.

Which heart you should lead is unclear. I would choose the 10. Partner will win the Ace if he has it. Hopefully, he will work out that I have done something unusual and will come to the right conclusion.

Incidentally, if my hand were:

♠ 8 6 2
♡ K Q J 10 8 6 2
◊ J 7 3
♣ —

I would lead the ♡2. This is unlikely to cost a trick and should certainly alert partner that something unusual is going on.

Note that you are not trying to fool anyone with this lead.

The thing to consider is that when you need partner to do something unusual, you have to make a lead which will wake him up. Not too difficult once you think of it. Obviously, since success will lead to a defeated contract, these unusual leads are quite worthwhile.

One point to make here. If you make one of these funny leads expecting that partner will do something for you, you better be sure that when you make a funny lead you have a good reason for it. If your partner does something silly because you got cute with your lead, you will end up with a confused and insecure partner. In which case, nothing you do will be believed.

A pair of very unusual and dangerous falsecards by the opening leader are shown by the following two actual examples:

Both vulnerable — South deals

♠ Q 10 5 4
♡ Q J 8
◊ 3
♣ A J 10 8 5

West	North	East	South
			1 NT
Pass	2 ◊ (1)	Pass	2 ♠
Pass	3 ♠ (2)	Pass	4 ♠
Pass	Pass	Pass	

(1) Game Forcing Stayman
(2) Slam try

This hand has lots of defensive potential and even though the opponents looked for slam, you can hope to beat 4♠.

What should you lead?

Spades are out, and you don't really want to lead a stiff diamond. Why try for a ruff with a natural trump trick?

Clubs are dangerous. You may have two tricks if you wait for them.

Hearts look far and away to be the best lead. The problem is that partner doesn't rate to have a heart honor. He may have one, but it's not likely. Best is to lead the ♡J.

The actual hand turned out to be:

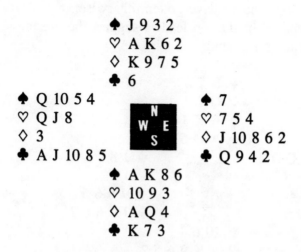

```
                    ♠ J 9 3 2
                    ♡ A K 6 2
                    ◊ K 9 7 5
                    ♣ 6
  ♠ Q 10 5 4                      ♠ 7
  ♡ Q J 8            N            ♡ 7 5 4
  ◊ 3             W     E         ◊ J 10 8 6 2
  ♣ A J 10 8 5       S            ♣ Q 9 4 2
                    ♠ A K 8 6
                    ♡ 10 9 3
                    ◊ A Q 4
                    ♣ K 7 3
```

Declarer won the ♡A and led a club to the king, and ace. West continued the ♡8 and declarer felt he couldn't afford to finesse. Down one.

East - West vulnerable — North deals.

♠ A Q 9 2
♡ 10 8 3
◊ Q 4 2
♣ 10 8 3

West	North	East	South
	1 ◊	Pass	1 ♡
Pass	2 NT	Pass	3 ♡
Pass	4 ♡	Pass	Pass
Pass			

On this sequence, there is a fair danger that dummy has a diamond suit. It may (no guarantee) be necessary to get your defensive tricks established quickly.

From your hand, spades look to be your best possibility.

Dummy rates to have the king, so you won't be giving declarer a trick he could never have gotten otherwise.

Which spade should you lead? I suggest the queen.

Here's the entire hand.

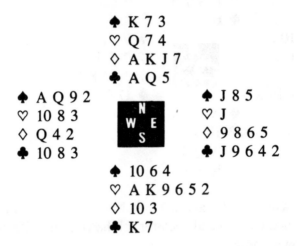

```
              ♠ K 7 3
              ♡ Q 7 4
              ◇ A K J 7
              ♣ A Q 5
♠ A Q 9 2                    ♠ J 8 5
♡ 10 8 3         N           ♡ J
◇ Q 4 2        W   E         ◇ 9 8 6 5
♣ 10 8 3         S           ♣ J 9 6 4 2
              ♠ 10 6 4
              ♡ A K 9 6 5 2
              ◇ 10 3
              ♣ K 7
```

The effect of the ♠Q in this case was spectacular. The queen won trick one. West led a second spade and declarer ducked to East's jack. Back to the ace. Now the final insult. West led his thirteenth spade and East ruffed it with the ♡J. West's ♡10 became the setting trick.

This lead worked out incredibly well. It need not have. It was, however, a reasonable effort.

Note that West chose this lead for a number of reasons.

1. The ♠K was marked in dummy and
2. No other suit looked promising.

The above lead is more likely to be found in books on deception than at the table.

More plausible is the lead of the queen, from say AQJ8 or AQJ10.

```
        ♠ K 7 3
        ♡ Q 7 4
        ◇ A K J 7
        ♣ A Q 5

           N
        W     E
           S

        ♠ 9 5 4
        ♡ A K 9 6 5 2
        ◇ 10 3
        ♣ K 7
```

If you were declaring 4♡ against the ♠Q lead, would you
cover, or would you duck, hoping for a doubleton or singleton
♠A on your right?

If West led from QJ1062, you have to duck the first round.
If West led from AQJ62, you better cover.

It's fair to say that declarer has a difficult guess. In practice, most declarers will duck in dummy, and that will be the
proper play most of the time.

Other Unusual Leads

A curiosity in the world of opening leads is this hand.

Both vulnerable — West deals

```
        ♠ A Q 10 8
        ♡ Q 6 4 2
        ◇ Q 9 3
        ♣ 7 2
```

West	North	East	South
Pass	1♣	Pass	1♡
Pass	2♡	Pass	2♠
Pass	3♡	Pass	4♡
Pass	Pass	Pass	

Any time you have a solid holding in declarer's second suit, you should consider leading trump. Even with four trumps to the queen, it should be safe. It may gain by cutting down ruffs and since declarer won't expect you to have led from Qxxx of trump, he probably won't guess the suit.

In fact, declarer is so unlikely to guess the trump, that you might try the lead solely to fool declarer.

North - South vulnerable — West deals.

♠ Q 6 4 2
♡ Q 8 3
◇ J 9 5
♣ 10 6 4

West	North	East	South
Pass	1♣	Pass	1◇
Pass	1♡	Pass	1♠
Pass	3♠	Pass	4 NT
Pass	5♡	Pass	6♠
Pass	Pass	Pass	

It would not be a bad idea to lead a trump (not the queen). Declarer has a 4-4 fit and with a trump lead, will probably play your partner for the ♠Q.

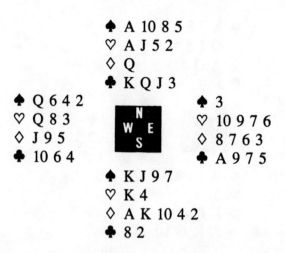

♠ A 10 8 5
♡ A J 5 2
◇ Q
♣ K Q J 3

♠ Q 6 4 2
♡ Q 8 3
◇ J 9 5
♣ 10 6 4

♠ 3
♡ 10 9 7 6
◇ 8 7 6 3
♣ A 9 7 5

♠ K J 9 7
♡ K 4
◇ A K 10 4 2
♣ 8 2

If you make a neutral lead, and on this hand, I don't know what that would be, declarer will try to guess spades. This he will do fifty percent of the time. With a spade lead, he will probably guess wrong far more than half the time.

You might try this trick at trick two as well.

East - West vulnerable — South deals.

♠ Q 6 4 2
♡ A K 7 3
◇ J 8 2
♣ 4 3

West	North	East	South
			1♣
Pass	1♡	Pass	1♠
Pass	4♠	Pass	4 NT
Pass	5◇	Pass	6♠
Pass	Pass	Pass	

```
              ♠ K J 8 7
              ♡ Q J 8 4 2
              ◇ A Q 5
              ♣ J
♠ Q 6 4 2              ♠ 3
♡ A K 7 3              ♡ 10 9 6
◇ J 8 2                ◇ 10 9 7 3
♣ 4 3                  ♣ 9 7 6 5 2
              ♠ A 10 9 5
              ♡ 5
              ◇ K 6 4
              ♣ A K Q 10 8
```

You cash the ♡K and switch to a . . . . .? If you switch
to a spade, declarer will misguess more often than not.

Chapter 2

DEFENDERS' FALSECARDS DURING PLAY

There are a variety of falsecards available to the defense. Some are even mandatory in that if you don't use them, you give declarer no losing option.

The Mandatory Defensive Falsecards

> *IMPORTANT NOTE:*
>
> In example diagrams, if a card has a star below it, it is the card led to the trick. The cards with an asterisk below are the remaining cards played to that trick.

```
                A J 8 2
                  *
K 3                            10 9 4
  *                               *
                Q 7 6 5
                    ★
```

East hopes declarer will return to his hand in order to lead the queen. That will produce a trick for East's ten spot.

```
                A J 8 2
K 4 3                          10 9
                Q 7 6 5
```

This is the holding East wants declarer to think exists.

```
                A J 8 2
                  *
K 3                            10 9 4
  *                               *
                Q 7 6 5
                    ★
```

If East fails to find the mandatory falsecard, declarer will have no choice but to play the ace. East must play the nine or ten in order to give declarer a losing option.

$$A\ J\ 8\ 2$$
*
$$K\ 3 \qquad\qquad\qquad 10\ 7\ 5$$
$$Q\ 8\ 6\ 4$$
★

This is a non-mandatory falsecard, in that declarer has a guess whether you play the five or the seven.

When faced with non-mandatory situations, you should follow some rules of thumb, such as:

1. Falsecard on even-numbered days.
2. Falsecard only in the majors
3. Falsecard only in the red suits
4. Play the card nearest your thumb

The main thing is not to become stereotyped as always falsecarding or never falsecarding.

$$A\ J\ 7$$
*
$$2 \qquad\qquad\qquad K\ 10\ 8\ 3$$
$$Q\ 9\ 6\ 5\ 4$$
★

If East fails to play the eight, declarer may guess the position anyway, but the eight should encourage declarer to come back to hand and lead the queen. If East started with 108 doubleton, the queen would lead to no losers and if East started with 8 singleton, the queen would hold declarer's losers to one.

These combinations are similar to the above combinations. The high cards have been changed, but the theme has not.

```
          A Q 8 2
            *
K 3                      10 9 5
  *                          *
          J 7 6 4
              ★
```

South may later lead the jack hoping East has 109 doubleton.

```
          A K 8 2
            *
Q 3                      10 9 5
  *                          *
          J 7 6 4
              ★
```

As above. If East plays the five, declarer will have no losing option. He will play the ace, and it will drop the queen.

The next three are all similar mandatory falsecards.

```
          K Q 10 2
            *
J 9 7 5                     4
    *                      *
          A 8 6 3
              ★
```

When West plays the nine, it gives declarer the option of playing either East or West for Jxxx. If West had played the five, declarer would have no choice but to play West for J9xx (if the suit turned out to be 4-1). If East had J9xx, he would have a sure trick.

```
          A Q 9 2
            *
10 8 6 5                   K
      *                    *
          J 7 4 3
              ★
```

Likewise, when West plays the eight, he gives declarer the option of playing East for K1065. Had West not played the eight, declarer would not play East for K108x because it would not be possible to pick up that combination. The idea with these holdings is to give declarer options that he *can* handle.

```
              K J 7 2
    6                        A 10 8 3

              Q 9 5 4
```

Likewise.

Another well known falsecard revolves around the specific defensive holding of Q10 or K10.

```
              J 9 2
    8 6 5                    K 10 ?

              A Q 7 4 3
```

If East plays the ten, declarer will finesse the queen and eventually will run the suit with no losers. But . . .

```
              J 9 2
    10 8 6 5                  K

              A Q 7 4 3
```

If East can convince declarer that this is the situation, then declarer may finesse the nine. This will work if West started with 10865, but will fail if East started with K10. Again, the defender creates an extra option for declarer.

```
              J 9 5
    7 6 3                    Q 10

              A K 8 4 2
```

This situation is virtually the same as when East held K10.

```
              Q 9 5
    8 6 3                    K 10

              A J 7 4 2
```

The K10 combination works just as well when the queen is

in dummy instead of the jack. It may be a little more nerve-racking for a defender to try the play, but it is still a sound effort.

You will note that these falsecards require that you defend in tempo. If East fumbles with his cards and plays a tentative king, it will be a wasted effort.

To some degree, a defender can do these things when declarer's hand and dummy are reversed. In theory, this should work.

A K 8 4 2 (Dummy)
＊
Q 10   7 6 3
＊   ＊
J 9 5
★

When South leads the five to the dummy, West can play the queen for the same result as discussed above. The problem is that declarer doesn't always have the right holding.

If the holdings were slightly different, say:

A K 8 4 2
Q 10   9 7 6 3
J 5
★

It would be quite silly for West to play the queen.

You should be aware that not all of these Q10 falsecards work. Declarer sometimes has a different holding than the one shown in the above examples.

Nonetheless, even when the situation is other than you hoped for, the trick often comes back.

```
          J 9 3
            *
K 7 5                Q 10
  *                    *
          A 8 6 4 2
            *
```

It looks here like declarer started with two losers and that your falsecard gave one back. In practice, declarer will not suspect the falsecard. He is more likely to lead to dummy's nine, hoping that East started with KQ doubleton.

```
          J 9 3
            *
A 4                  Q 10
  *                    *
          K 8 7 6 5 2
            *
```

Again, it looks like declarer has two losers if the defense played straightforward cards. But as often happens, the trick comes back. Declarer will expect East to have started with a stiff queen and will finesse into the ten.

```
          J 9 3
            *
A                    Q 10
  *                    *
          K 8 7 6 5 4 2
            *
```

OK. We pay off to this one.

Defensively, the Q10 combination offers all kinds of chances to falsecard.

```
          A K J 9 4 2
            *
7 6 5                Q 10
  *                    *
          8 3
            *
```

If East can play the queen without thought, declarer is very likely to finesse later into the ten. It's true that if East followed with the ten, he might still score his queen, but then, maybe not. I think the falsecard is the winner more often than not.

```
            A K J 9 3
7 6 5          ♣              Q 10
   ♣                            ♣
            8 4 2
               ♣
```

Note that when dummy has a five-card suit, the queen falsecard is not as effective. Declarer, if you drop the queen, can play the king next to see if you were really serious. If so, he can still finesse against your partner's ten.

```
            A 2
Q 10         ♣              7 5 4
 ♣                            ♣
            K J 9 8 6 3
               ♣
```

This suit comes up quite frequently. Often it is the trump suit. The queen falsecard may fool declarer into finessing into the ten.

```
            K 7 3
Q 10         ♣              9 6 2
 ♣                            ♣
            A J 8 5 4
               ♠
```

Here the effect is the same except that declarer may try finessing against your partner's hypothetical 10962.

```
            K 7 3
Q                          10 9 6 2
            A J 8 5 4
               ♠
```

This is the situation you are trying to imitate.

```
            K 7 3
Q 9          ♠              10 6 2
 ♣                            ♣
            A J 8 5 4
               ♠
```

This is a possible extension of the above. I have never seen anyone try falsecarding in this situation with Q9 instead of Q10, but it's possible.

```
              K J 9 8 3
                 ♣
Q 10                           7 5 4
  ♣                               ♣
              A 6 2
                 ♠
```

Once again, the play of the queen leaves declarer with the very real option of finessing against East's ten. If East started with 10754, it would be necessary.

Note that these falsecards only work when declarer has no clue as to your distribution. If, in the preceding example, West had opened 1 NT, no declarer would go for this particular falsecard.

These positions are a little unlikely, but they have potential.

```
              10 8 2
                 ★
A 5 4                          Q 9
  ♣                              ♣
              K J 7 6 3
                 ♣
```

Declarer may finesse into East's nine.

```
              10 8 2
                 ★
K 5 4                          Q 9
  ♣                              ♣
              A J 7 6 3
                 ♣
```

If this is the setup, declarer will be less inclined to finesse into the nine. East's play of the queen could be from KQ9 so unless declarer suspects a bad break, he won't fall for this falsecard.

```
              10 8 2
                 ★
A 3                            Q 9
  ♣                              ♣
              K J 7 6 5 4
                 ♣
```

This would be a poor time to falsecard. You should try this only when you think declarer has a five-card suit.

Note that East can try the above falsecards from K9 as well as Q9.

```
              10 8 2
                 *
Q 5 4                      K 9
   *                         *
              A J 7 6 3
                 *
```

East may get his nine spot if declarer misjudges.

The J9 Falsecards

One of the more intriguing set of falsecards occurs when a defender has the J9 of a suit.

```
              Q 10 8 6 2

              A 4
```

As declarer, you lead the ace, catching the three from West and the nine from East. When you lead the four, West plays the five. Should you play the queen or the ten? (Assume you need four tricks.)

If you believe the suit is divided 4-2, your correct play is the queen. If East has K9, you can't run the suit no matter what you do. If East has the J9, you can get four tricks by playing the queen. Go for the maximum.

Some years ago the *Bridge World* had a long article on what East should play on your ace if he holds K93. If he plays the nine, declarer may be lured into playing dummy's queen on the rationale described above.

It is true a good defender will play the nine from K92. It is also true that there aren't that many good defenders.

Let's go back to the original suit, i.e.,

```
              Q 10 8 6 2

              A 4
```

39

Let's say that when declarer plays the ace, East drops the jack. Wouldn't you, as declarer, be inclined to finesse dummy's eight, hoping East has KJ?

If you agree, then you will also agree that an excellent play by East would be to play the J from J9 doubleton.

These situations are examples of what a defender can do with J9.

                    Q 10 8 6 2
                        *
    K 7 5 3   J 9
        *   *
                    A 4
                      ★

East hopes declarer will finesse the eight

                    A 10 8 6 3
                        *
    Q 5 4 2   J 9
        *   *
                    K 7
                      ★

East hopes declarer will finesse the eight. Without the falsecard, declarer might play the king, ace, dropping the J9 and can then concede one trick to West's queen.

                    A 10 8 6 3
                        *
    J 5 4 2   Q 9
        *   *
                    K 7
                      ★

A possible extension of the previous example. This falsecard is a bit dangerous because declarer may have KJ5 (for example).

                    Q 3
                      *
    J 9   K 6 2
      *   *
                    A 10 8 7 5 4
                          ★

Again, hoping declarer will finesse into the nine.

```
              A 8 3
               *
K 7 5                    J 9
 *                        *
              Q 10 6 4 2
                 *
```

Declarer may lose to East's nine. Note how easy it is for declarer to misguess these combinations. At the table, these falsecards are frequently overlooked. That's why most players are unfamiliar with them. That's a shame because they are very effective and deservedly so.

```
              10 7 2
                *
  K 5 3                  J 9
   *                      *
              A Q 8 6 4
                 *
```

Will East score his nine?

```
              A Q 8 6 4
                 *
 J 9                     K 5 3
              10 7 2
                *
```

It's dangerous for West to falsecard the jack. That would lose a trick whenever declarer had 102 and East K753. It could work though, if West knows, somehow, that South has three cards in this suit, the jack will be a good try.

Other J9 Combinations

Sometimes you have a higher honor with your J9. Usually, for purposes of falsecards, it will be the ace. Here are a few additional falsecards.

```
              K 10 7 3
                 *
  A J 9                  6 5 2
    *                      *
              Q 8 4
                *
```

In these two combinations, declarer may take a finesse into West's nine.

```
                K Q 7 6 4
    A J 9                         3 2
                10 8 5
                ─────────────────
                10 8 7 6
    5 3 2                         A J 9
                K Q 4
```

This combination takes a little longer to develop, but it will eventually. Declarer may lead the queen to East's ace and finesse the eight on the third round of the suit.

Note this won't work if declarer has enough entries to dummy to lead through East a second time. Especially note that West must be alert to what's going on. If he discards one of his small cards ("I had only three little ones partner") then East's deception will be wasted.

```
                K 8 4 2
    6 5 3                         A J 9
                Q 10 7
```

This combination also takes three tricks to develop. West better hold on to his 653 in order to give the falsecard a fair chance.

Faking Your Holding

One common and effective defensive falsecard is to mislead declarer as to your holding in a suit. This can be done in two ways.

1. You can refuse to win a trick when it was possible to have done so.
2. You can win with an unusual card which makes it appear that you don't have a different card.

There are many reasons why you might try one of these tactics.

```
                    K Q 10 5
                      *
        J 9 3                       A 7 4
          *                           *
                    8 6 2
                      ★
```

If there are entries to the South hand, by playing low on the first trick East is hoping that declarer will simply misguess the suit. If declarer later leads to the queen, the defense will come to two tricks when they might have gotten just one. In this case, you are hoping to mislead declarer, i.e., you are falsecarding.

You might duck the ace in the above combination for tactical reasons.

North - South vulnerable — East deals.

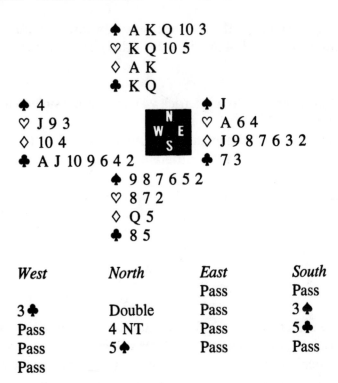

```
                    ♠ A K Q 10 3
                    ♡ K Q 10 5
                    ◊ A K
                    ♣ K Q
  ♠ 4                              ♠ J
  ♡ J 9 3                          ♡ A 6 4
  ◊ 10 4                           ◊ J 9 8 7 6 3 2
  ♣ A J 10 9 6 4 2                 ♣ 7 3
                    ♠ 9 8 7 6 5 2
                    ♡ 8 7 2
                    ◊ Q 5
                    ♣ 8 5
```

West	North	East	South
		Pass	Pass
3♣	Double	Pass	3♠
Pass	4 NT	Pass	5♣
Pass	5♠	Pass	Pass
Pass			

West leads the ♣A and continues a club to dummy's king. The trump ace draws trumps followed by the ◊AK. Declarer comes to his hand for the last time with a spade and leads a heart in this position.

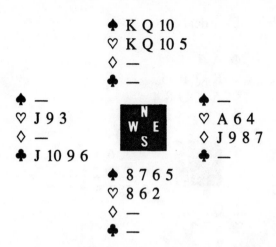

♠ K Q 10
♥ K Q 10 5
♦ —
♣ —

♠ —
♥ J 9 3
♦ —
♣ J 10 9 6

N
W E
S

♠ —
♥ A 6 4
♦ J 9 8 7
♣ —

♠ 8 7 6 5
♥ 8 6 2
♦ —
♣ —

If declarer thinks West had a doubleton heart, he should play the king as it caters to West having Ax or Jx.

If declarer thinks West has three hearts, he should hook the 10 since there is no reentry for a second heart play.

In practice, declarer misguessed the position and played the king. Even with declarer's misguess, he would have succeeded if East had taken the trick as the defense would have been end-played. But, by refusing the trick, East left dummy on lead and there was no way now to avoid two heart losers.

Note that in the example hand, East was not trying to fool anyone by ducking. He was just using good technique.

Likewise.

Both vulnerable — East deals.

```
              ♠ A 5
              ♡ K Q 10 5
              ◊ A K Q 8 4
              ♣ J 2
   ♠ K J 8 7 2            ♠ 10 4 3
   ♡ J 9 3         N      ♡ A 6 4
   ◊ 9 3        W   E     ◊ J 10 2
   ♣ K 10 7        S      ♣ Q 9 5 4
              ♠ Q 9 6
              ♡ 8 7 2
              ◊ 7 6 5
              ♣ A 8 6 3
```

West	North	East	South
		Pass	Pass
Pass	1 ◊	Pass	1 NT
Pass	3 NT	Pass	Pass
Pass			

West led the ♠7 to declarer's queen. If the diamonds break, declarer has nine tricks by establishing a heart trick. Declarer wasn't greedy so he led to the ♡K rather than chance finessing the ten.

Sound technique now requires East to duck. Declarer can't come back to his hand except in clubs and that would establish three of four club tricks for the defense.

If East takes his ♡A, he runs the risk that declarer will find some extra courage and risk finessing the ♡10.

Why give declarer an option that works?

Conversely, if East held ♡AJ3, he should take the ace and clear the spades. Now declarer has the option of finessing in hearts, but it would be a losing option.

North
A Q J 10   *East*
            K 5 2

There are various reasons why you might duck when declarer takes a finesse.

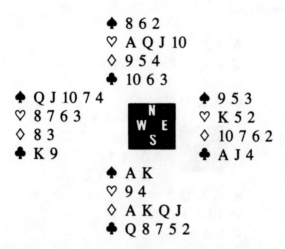

♠ 8 6 2
♡ A Q J 10
◇ 9 5 4
♣ 10 6 3

♠ Q J 10 7 4   ♠ 9 5 3
♡ 8 7 6 3   ♡ K 5 2
◇ 8 3   ◇ 10 7 6 2
♣ K 9   ♣ A J 4

♠ A K
♡ 9 4
◇ A K Q J
♣ Q 8 7 5 2

South plays 3 NT with the ♠Q lead. South wins and leads the ♡4 to the queen. If East and West use count signals, West will echo with the seven or eight and East will infer that declarer has two hearts, exactly. By ducking the first heart, East will hold declarer to one or two heart tricks according to whether declarer finesses again.

It's possible that East might refuse the trick twice!

          A Q J 10
9 7 3   K 6 2
          8 5 4

If East is sure declarer has exactly three cards in this suit, he can duck the first two finesses and take the third. This will be effective more often than you might expect. Be sure of two things before you try this ploy.

1. You must know declarer has three cards in the suit.
2. You must know declarer has enough entries to repeat the finesse three times. If declarer can't get back to his hand, then his only recourse will be to drop the king.

A third common reason for ducking is that you want declarer to misuse his entries.

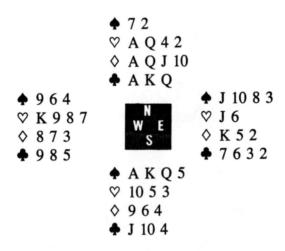

```
                    ♠ 7 2
                    ♡ A Q 4 2
                    ◊ A Q J 10
                    ♣ A K Q
    ♠ 9 6 4                        ♠ J 10 8 3
    ♡ K 9 8 7          N           ♡ J 6
    ◊ 8 7 3         W     E        ◊ K 5 2
    ♣ 9 8 5            S           ♣ 7 6 3 2
                    ♠ A K Q 5
                    ♡ 10 5 3
                    ◊ 9 6 4
                    ♣ J 10 4
```

Against 3 NT, West leads the ♣9. Declarer wins and enters his hand with a spade in order to finesse in diamonds. If East wins, declarer will use his last entry to take the winning heart finesse. If East ducks the diamond, declarer is likely to use his last entry to repeat the diamond finesse. Maybe he will, maybe he won't.

At least he has the option.

An extention of this suit is the following:

$$\text{A Q J 10 8 6 2}$$
$$\underset{*}{9} \qquad\qquad\qquad \text{K 4}$$
$$\underset{*}{3}$$

If dummy has no side entry, it would be wise for East to duck this trick.

Now it would be foolish of East to duck if West had a singleton and it would be foolish to duck if West had three small.

```
              A Q J 10 8 6 2
  x x x                         K 4
              x
```

— or —

```
              A Q J 10 8 6 2
  x                             K x
              x x x
```

Both of these circumstances would be embarrassing to East if declarer finessed the queen and East ducked.

In order to avoid this problem, West must give count when he doesn't have the king so that East will duck when it's correct.

And, when West does have the king, he should echo as if he had a doubleton.

```
              A Q J 10 8 6 2
                            *
  K 7 3                          5
    *                            *
              9 4
              *
```

After the nine wins, declarer may be suspicious when he leads the four and West plays the three. Perhaps he will suspect East of ducking with K5.

As they say, nothing ventured . . . . .

Once in a while, this will be the set up and you will wish you had never read this book.

```
              A Q J 10 8 6 2
                            *
  7                              K 4
  *                              *
              9 5 3
              *
```

East will think West had either 75 or 73 and East will duck smoothly on that assumption. Alas.

Other common suit combinations where a defender may refuse to win a trick are:

```
              A K J 10 2
                  ♣
    8                        Q 7 6 3
    ♣                            ♣
              5
              ♠
   ─────────────────────────────────
              A K J 10 2
                  ♣
    4                        Q 7 3
    ♣                            ♣
              9
              ♠
```

This one is a bit nervewracking. Don't try this if dummy has a side entry. The main reason for ducking is to keep declarer from getting four tricks. If declarer has entries to dummy, it won't help East to duck his queen.

Incidentally, you should be sure when you refuse a trick that you have nothing better to do. For example:

East - West vulnerable — East deals.

```
              ♠ 7 3
              ♡ 7 2
              ◇ A Q J 10 8 6 5
              ♣ K 4
                              ♠ K 9 8 2
              N               ♡ 10 6 3
            W   E             ◇ K 9 2
              S               ♣ 8 5 2
```

West	North	East	South
		Pass	1 ♣
Pass	1 ◇	Pass	1 ♠
Pass	3 ◇	Pass	3 NT
Pass	Pass	Pass	

Partner leads the ♡8 (fourth best) to your ten and declarer's jack. Declarer finesses the ♢Q (7, 4, Q, ?). Do you duck? You should grab it. This is not a good time to be tricky. Partner's ♡8 tells you declarer has two higher hearts, one of which is the jack. Also, from the auction, you know declarer has three hearts or fewer.

Here are some possible heart combinations.

```
                72
   A K 9 8 4              10 6 3
                Q J 5
```

Possible. Partner might lead the eight.

```
                72
   A Q 9 8 4              10 6 3
                K J 5
```

Partner certainly would lead the eight.

```
                72
   A K Q 8 4              10 6 3
                J 9 5
```

Nonsense — can't exist.

```
                72
   K Q 9 8 4              10 6 3
                A J 5
```

Not likely. The king would be led from this holding.

If you trust these observations, you can win the first diamond and return a heart. Partner's hearts are ready to run.

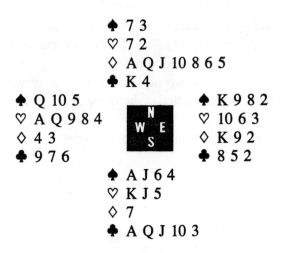

♠ 7 3
♡ 7 2
◇ A Q J 10 8 6 5
♣ K 4

♠ Q 10 5   ♠ K 9 8 2
♡ A Q 9 8 4   ♡ 10 6 3
◇ 4 3   ◇ K 9 2
♣ 9 7 6   ♣ 8 5 2

♠ A J 6 4
♡ K J 5
◇ 7
♣ A Q J 10 3

If the defense had been hung up on fooling declarer, he would have cashed out his nine winners.

K Q 10 2
5   A J 3
9

Slightly unusual but almost sure to work.

K Q 10 9 2
5   A J 3
4

Far more common than the above and almost always defended correctly.

A Q 10 9 8
6   K J 4 2
3

Ducking here can hold declarer to two tricks. You should not do this if declarer has *no* side entries to dummy. In this case, he is only getting one trick. No need to give him two.

No one vulnerable — North deals

```
              ♠ A Q 9 7 6
              ♡ A 7 2
              ◊ 5 4
              ♣ 7 6 4
                              ♠ K 8 4 2
                              ♡ Q 8 3
         N                    ◊ 10 6 3 2
       W   E                  ♣ Q 2
         S
```

West	North	East	South
	Pass	Pass	1 NT
Pass	3♠	Pass	3 NT
Pass	Pass	Pass	

West leads the ♡ 10 to your queen and South's king. South leads the ♠ 10 covered by West's jack and dummy's queen.

If you take this declarer will later set up the spade suit and the ♡ A will be an entry.

By ducking, you can hold declarer to two spade tricks. This may or may not defeat declarer, but it will certainly make it more difficult for him.

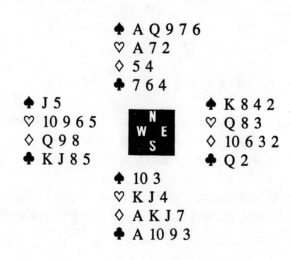

```
              ♠ A Q 9 7 6
              ♡ A 7 2
              ◊ 5 4
              ♣ 7 6 4
♠ J 5                         ♠ K 8 4 2
♡ 10 9 6 5        N           ♡ Q 8 3
◊ Q 9 8        W   E          ◊ 10 6 3 2
♣ K J 8 5        S            ♣ Q 2
              ♠ 10 3
              ♡ K J 4
              ◊ A K J 7
              ♣ A 10 9 3
```

Declarer can make 3 NT easily enough if he guesses everything. But he may not.

Actually, if declarer played properly, he would make 3 NT without guessing. If South just ducks when West plays the ♠J, he can bring home three spade tricks against any defense.

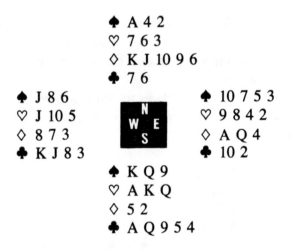

K J 10 9 6

3   A Q 4   ?

2

In this common holding, the correct play usually is to win and go about whatever you were doing. There are exceptions, of course.

You might let declarer win the trick in order to hinder his establishing the suit.

```
              ♠ A 4 2
              ♡ 7 6 3
              ◊ K J 10 9 6
              ♣ 7 6
  ♠ J 8 6                    ♠ 10 7 5 3
  ♡ J 10 5        N          ♡ 9 8 4 2
  ◊ 8 7 3       W   E        ◊ A Q 4
  ♣ K J 8 3       S          ♣ 10 2
              ♠ K Q 9
              ♡ A K Q
              ◊ 5 2
              ♣ A Q 9 5 4
```

Declarer plays 3 NT with the ♡J lead. His normal play is to finesse the ◊9. If East wins with the queen, declarer will be able to set up the diamonds and will come to at least ten tricks.

If East ducks the diamond, declarer won't have entries to set up and use the suit. He will probably end up with eight tricks.

K J 10 9 6

3   A Q 4   ?

2

The second possible falsecard with this combination is to win with the ace. There are a number of reasons why you might do this.

1. If declarer thinks this finesse is working, he might try it again when he could have taken a different finesse instead. (See page 48.)
2. Declarer, thinking this suit is running, might not hold up in a dangerous suit.

North - South vulnerable — North deals.

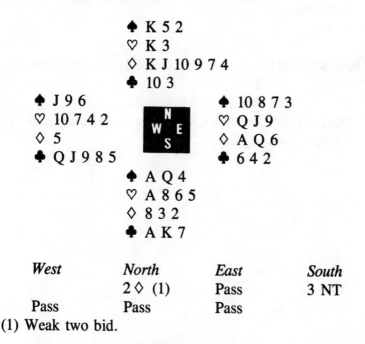

♠	K 5 2
♡	K 3
◇	K J 10 9 7 4
♣	10 3

♠ J 9 6   ♠ 10 8 7 3
♡ 10 7 4 2   ♡ Q J 9
◇ 5   ◇ A Q 6
♣ Q J 9 8 5   ♣ 6 4 2

♠ A Q 4
♡ A 8 6 5
◇ 8 3 2
♣ A K 7

West	*North*	*East*	*South*
	2 ◇ (1)	Pass	3 NT
Pass	Pass	Pass	

(1) Weak two bid.

West leads the ♣ Q to South's ace. At trick two, South leads the ◇ 8 to the five, four, and ?

If East wins the queen and returns a club, declarer will duck and win the next club. When he loses to the $\Diamond$ A, the defense will be through because East will have run out of clubs. Ten tricks to South.

The result will be the same if East ducks the first diamond. When declarer leads the second diamond, he will see what has occurred and he will be forced into holding up in clubs. Again, ten tricks.

If East wins the first diamond trick with the ace, he may lull declarer into a false sense of security. Declarer may think the diamonds are all good. If so, he may win East's club return immediately, and that will be a disaster. Instead of twelve tricks,

    3 spades
    2 hearts
    5 diamonds
    2 clubs,

declarer will find he has only one diamond trick and hence only eight tricks.

3.   Declarer, thinking a suit is running, may be talked out of taking a winning finesse.

North - South vulnerable — East deals

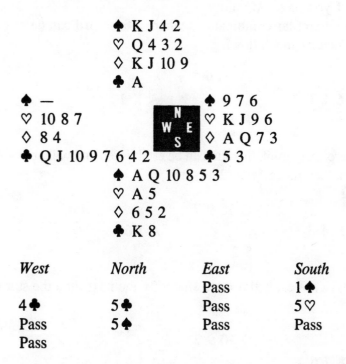

| ♠ K J 4 2 |
| ♡ Q 4 3 2 |
| ◇ K J 10 9 |
| ♣ A |

West	North	East	South
		Pass	1♠
4♣	5♣	Pass	5♡
Pass	5♠	Pass	Pass
Pass			

West leads the ♣Q to dummy's ace. South draws three rounds of trumps and finesses the ◇J (2, 8, J, ?).

Well? East knows declarer has six spade tricks, the ♡A, two diamonds, eventually, and two clubs.

If East wins the ◇Q and leads a heart, declarer will have no choice but to finesse. But if East wins the ◇A and leads a heart, declarer may rise with the ace, thinking the diamonds will provide discards.

At IMPs, this should not work because declarer can guarantee eleven tricks by finessing the heart lead. At matchpoints, though, greed does strange things to people and this falsecard should work.

Incidentally, it is not necessary for a defender to have AQx(x) in order to make this falsecard.

If the falsecard is going to work, it should be just as effective if you have AQ alone.

Other similar combinations where a falsecard can be effective include the following:

Q 10 9 7 5

6 4 3   A K J

8 2

Declarer may think this suit can be established and will not work on another more favorable suit.

Q 10 9 7 5

K 4 3   A J 6

8 2

Likewise. West better duck smoothly the next time the suit is led.

Q 10 9 2

8 7 6   A J 5

K 4 3

Declarer may be talked out of a different finesse thinking this one is working. (See page 48.)

A Q J 9 2

5 4   K 10 8 7

6 3

Declarer may not have the entries to set up this suit.

```
              A Q 10 9
                   *
7 5 4 (3)                      K J 3 (K J)
    *                            *
              8 6 2
                 ★
```

Another example of giving declarer a false sense of security. If he thinks he has three tricks in this suit, he may be talked out of a productive alternative.

```
              A J 9 8 2
                 *
6 4                            K Q 10 5
  *                               *
              7 3
                ★
```

Give declarer hope that the suit is coming home.

```
              K J 10 3
                  *
8 6 4                          Q 9 7
    *                              *
              A 5 2
                 ★
```

If declarer now plays the ace and hooks the jack, you may hold declarer to two tricks if dummy has no entry.

```
              K J 10 6 3
                  *
A 5 2                          Q 9 8
    *                              *
              7 4
                ★
```

This may cause declarer to use an entry to finesse this suit when his entry could have been better used elsewhere. Also, it's possible that declarer won't be able to set up the suit at all if dummy has insufficient entries (assuming declarer misguesses this suit when he leads the seven to dummy.) (See the hand on page 53.)

A small and relatively unknown family of falsecards occurs when declarer has played a suit correctly. Even though declarer is going to get the maximum number of tricks, you may be able to make him work a little harder to get them.

```
              K J 9 2
Q 8 5                      10 6 3
              A 7 4
```

Declarer plays the ace and leads to the jack. If East drops the ten, declarer may use an entry back to his hand to take another finesse.

```
              Q 10 7 2
  K 8 5                    J 9 4
              A 6 3
```

Likewise. Declarer plays the ace and leads to the queen. This is declarer's best guess, but there is no reason for the defense to go quietly. If East drops the jack on the queen, declarer may think the suit looks like this.

```
              Q 10 7 2
  K 9 8 5                  J 4
              A 6 3
```

If so, declarer will either look elsewhere or will squander an entry in order to lead toward dummy's ten.

```
              K J 8 7 4 2
                *
  A 10                     Q 9
    *                       *
              6 5 3
                ★
```

Still another example of misrepresenting the actual lie of the cards. Declarer can lead a low card from dummy now, but it's possible he will try something else.

                    A K 10 3
Q 9 5   J 8 4
                    7 6 2

If South plays the ace and king, it may slow South down if East
drops the jack. West *could* have Q985 and South may not wish
to risk leading low from dummy.

                    A Q 10 8 2
K 3   J 9

                    7 6 5 4

What declarer would trust this suit to divide if he could somehow
repeat the finesse.

You could try this variation.

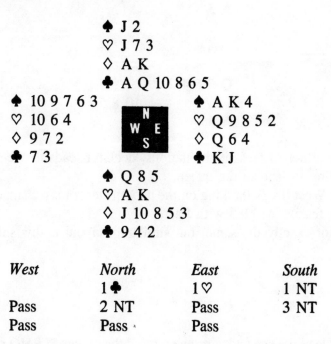

```
                    ♠ J 2
                    ♡ J 7 3
                    ◊ A K
                    ♣ A Q 10 8 6 5
    ♠ 10 9 7 6 3                 ♠ A K 4
    ♡ 10 6 4          N          ♡ Q 9 8 5 2
    ◊ 9 7 2       W     E        ◊ Q 6 4
    ♣ 7 3            S           ♣ K J
                    ♠ Q 8 5
                    ♡ A K
                    ◊ J 10 8 5 3
                    ♣ 9 4 2
```

West	North	East	South
	1 ♣	1 ♡	1 NT
Pass	2 NT	Pass	3 NT
Pass	Pass	Pass	

West led the ♡4 to South's king (4, 3, 8, K). South now
finessed the ♣Q, which won! East's jack looked like a singleton

so declarer came back to his $\heartsuit$ A and finessed clubs again. Down two.

$$\text{A K Q 3}$$
$$\text{9 5 2} \qquad\qquad \text{J 8 7}$$
$$\text{10 6 4}$$

When dummy plays the ace and king, East throws the jack. Declarer, fearing 9852 with West may come to his ten spot. This could create entry problems.

A classic and very effective falsecard, intended to talk declarer out of the winning line, is the following.

$$\text{Q 7 6 4 2}$$
$$\text{K J 10} \qquad\qquad \text{9 8 5}$$
$$\text{A 3}$$

or

$$\text{Q 7 6 4 2}$$
$$\text{K J 9} \qquad\qquad \text{10 8 5}$$
$$\text{A 3}$$

In either of these combinations, declarer leads the ace, intending to lead to the queen.

If West drops the king on the ace, declarer may change his plan fearing J10985 with East.

Not exactly the same, but similar in layout is this suit.

$$\text{A 5 3}$$

$$\text{Q 9 7 6 2}$$

You lead the ace and continue toward the queen. If RHO plays the jack or ten on the second round, it is possible to play low from your hand, hoping for Kx with West.

This opens up the possibility that East, with KJx or K10x, should duck the second trick.

```
              A 5 3
   10 4                   K J 8
              Q 9 7 6 2
   ─────────────────────────────
              A 5 3
   J 4                    K 10 8
              Q 9 7 6 2
```

This works more frequently than one might imagine. Also, since it is the most common falsecard around, you will have many opportunities to use it.

Also similar are the following:

```
              Q 10 7 2
   K 8 6                  J 9 3
              A 5 4
```

On declarer's ace, West drops the king. He may do this for a couple of reasons. One reason might be to discourage declarer from pursuing the suit. Another reason might be that West wants to get his partner in. If East truly has Jxx, it will be an entry if declarer tries to set up the suit.

```
              Q 10 7 3 2
   K 6                    J 9 8
              A 5 4
```

The same reasoning could apply here too.

The last and extreme example in this format is this remarkable case.

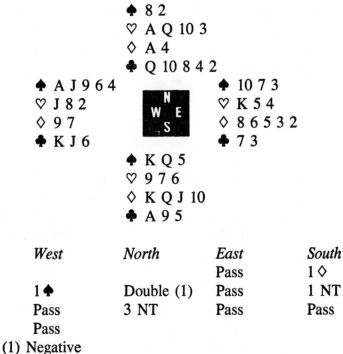

Q 10 8 4 2
K J 6   7 3
A 9 5

West desperately wants his partner to get in and at the same time doesn't want declarer to pursue this suit. By dropping the king, West may convince declarer that East has the guarded jack.

Both vulnerable — East deals.

♠ 8 2
♡ A Q 10 3
◊ A 4
♣ Q 10 8 4 2

♠ A J 9 6 4   ♠ 10 7 3
♡ J 8 2   ♡ K 5 4
◊ 9 7   ◊ 8 6 5 3 2
♣ K J 6   ♣ 7 3

♠ K Q 5
♡ 9 7 6
◊ K Q J 10
♣ A 9 5

West	North	East	South
		Pass	1 ◊
1 ♠	Double (1)	Pass	1 NT
Pass	3 NT	Pass	Pass
Pass			

(1) Negative

   West leads the ♠6 to the ten and queen. When declarer plays the ♣A, West drops the king. This gives declarer an eighth trick, but since it looks like East has the ♣J, declarer can't play clubs for his ninth trick. Instead, declarer tries the heart finesse. One down.

Faking Strength in Order to Gain Tricks

There are a few falsecards where your intention is to gain a trick rather than to hinder declarer's progress.

<pre>
            Q 8 2
   5   K J 4 3
            A 10 9 7 6
</pre>

If declarer plays the ten to the queen, and East ducks, declarer may think the suit is splitting. He may play the ace next and thus lose two tricks.

<pre>
            Q 10 3
   5 4 2   K J 6
            A 9 8 7
</pre>

This is quite likely to persuade declarer to take a second finesse against West's jack.

In very similar fashion

<pre>
            Q 10 4 3
   5   K J 6 2
            A 9 8 7
</pre>

If declarer ruffs something with the ten, East may gain a trick by overruffing with the king rather than the jack. South may play West for the jack.

North - South vulnerable — South deals

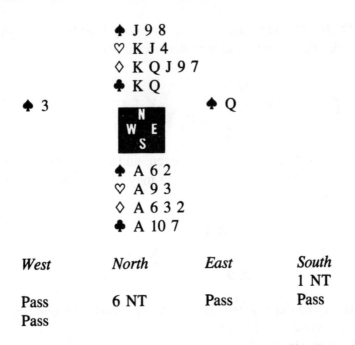

♠ J 9 8
♡ K J 4
◊ K Q J 9 7
♣ K Q

♠ 3

♠ Q

♠ A 6 2
♡ A 9 3
◊ A 6 3 2
♣ A 10 7

West	North	East	South
			1 NT
Pass	6 NT	Pass	Pass
Pass			

West leads the ♠3 to the eight, queen, ace. Where should you look for your twelfth trick? Should you hook the ♡J or the ♠9?

If you think the ♠9, here is the complete hand.

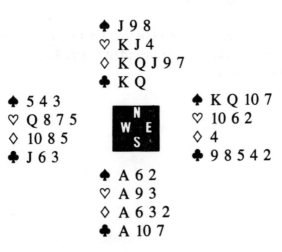

♠ J 9 8
♡ K J 4
◊ K Q J 9 7
♣ K Q

♠ 5 4 3
♡ Q 8 7 5
◊ 10 8 5
♣ J 6 3

♠ K Q 10 7
♡ 10 6 2
◊ 4
♣ 9 8 5 4 2

♠ A 6 2
♡ A 9 3
◊ A 6 3 2
♣ A 10 7

I would finesse the spade too.

The same play can be made with a completely different purpose.

North - South vulnerable — South deals

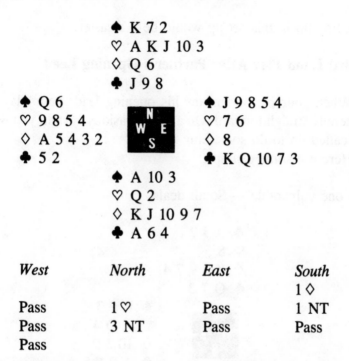

♠ K 7 2
♡ A K J 10 3
◊ Q 6
♣ J 9 8

♠ Q 6
♡ 9 8 5 4
◊ A 5 4 3 2
♣ 5 2

♠ J 9 8 5 4
♡ 7 6
◊ 8
♣ K Q 10 7 3

♠ A 10 3
♡ Q 2
◊ K J 10 9 7
♣ A 6 4

West	North	East	South
			1 ◊
Pass	1 ♡	Pass	1 NT
Pass	3 NT	Pass	Pass
Pass			

West had an awkward choice of leads. Deciding that East could have overcalled 1 ♠ with a decent suit, West led the ♣ 5.

When East played the queen, declarer was quick to take the trick. Now when West won his ◊ A, another club set the contract.

Had East played the ♣ 10, declarer might have held up. With East's actual play of the queen, it would have been very dangerous for declarer to hold up.

This could have been the club suit.

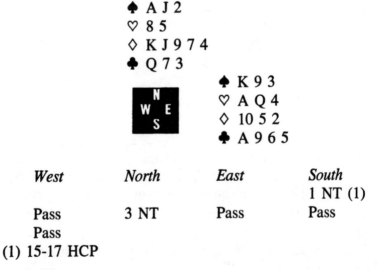

```
              J 9 8
K 10 7 5 3                Q 2
              A 6 4
```

Holding up in this set up would be a disaster.

Third Hand Play After Partner's Opening Lead

When your partner makes his opening lead, your play is generally straightforward. On a few occasions though, you will be called on to do something unusual.

Here are some examples:

No one vulnerable — South deals

```
        ♠ A J 2
        ♡ 8 5
        ◊ K J 9 7 4
        ♣ Q 7 3
              N          ♠ K 9 3
            W   E        ♡ A Q 4
              S          ◊ 10 5 2
                         ♣ A 9 6 5
```

West	North	East	South
			1 NT (1)
Pass	3 NT	Pass	Pass
Pass			

(1) 15-17 HCP

Partner leads the ♡6. Standard play here is to win the ace and return the queen. The problem with this is that declarer may hold up one round. Then when you get in, you will have no heart to return.

The solution is to play the ♡Q at trick one. Declarer will almost surely have to take this trick since he will be afraid your partner has the ♡A. Now, when you get in, you will be able to continue hearts by leading the ace and four.

Any time you try a falsecard, you have to be aware of possible bad consequences.

Are there any here?

In this case, there are none. If partner has the ♡K, it doesn't matter whether you play AQ or QA. Notice, incidentally, that on this hand, your partner has a maximum of one point if the opponents's 1 NT is 15 to 17 as advertised.

If partner's one point is the ♡J, you should get the heart suit going by playing the queen first. If partner's hearts are headed by the ten, so that declarer has KJ(x), then you weren't going to run them in any event.

Does this mean that with AQx of partner's lead you should always play the queen?

Absolutely not.

The key to this play is whether you think you or your partner will get in next.

In the example hand, the auction and the dummy told you the opponents had at least 26 HCP. From your hand, you knew your partner wasn't getting in.

Compare this next hand with the above hand.

No one vulnerable — South deals

```
              ♠ A J 2
              ♡ 8 5
              ◊ K J 9 7 4
              ♣ Q 7 3
                                    ♠ 10 9 3
                    N               ♡ A Q 4
                W       E           ◊ 10 5 2
                    S               ♣ 10 8 6 5
```

West	North	East	South
			1 NT
Pass	3 NT	Pass	Pass
Pass			

West leads the ♡6 just like on the previous hand.

Your correct play here is the ace and queen. If the heart suit is running, it doesn't matter how you play them, but if declarer has the king, you have to play the ace and queen so that partner will know what's happening when he gets in.

From partner's point of view, this might be the heart suit:

```
                    8 5
                     *
       J 9 7 6 2           Q 4 3
            *                *
                  A K 10
                    *
```

When partner gets in, he won't be sure a heart is safe. Declarer could have the AK10 which is consistent with what he has seen.

If this is so, it would be silly to continue hearts.

Here are the two complete hands.

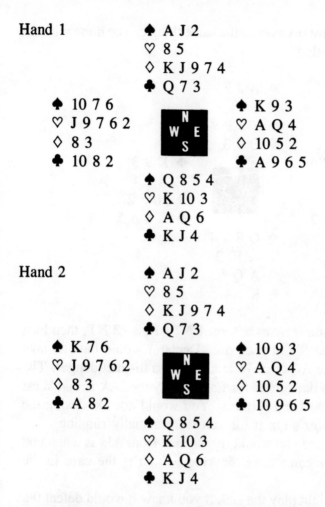

Hand 1

```
                    ♠ A J 2
                    ♡ 8 5
                    ◇ K J 9 7 4
                    ♣ Q 7 3
♠ 10 7 6                              ♠ K 9 3
♡ J 9 7 6 2          N               ♡ A Q 4
◇ 8 3             W     E             ◇ 10 5 2
♣ 10 8 2             S               ♣ A 9 6 5
                    ♠ Q 8 5 4
                    ♡ K 10 3
                    ◇ A Q 6
                    ♣ K J 4
```

Hand 2

```
                    ♠ A J 2
                    ♡ 8 5
                    ◇ K J 9 7 4
                    ♣ Q 7 3
♠ K 7 6                              ♠ 10 9 3
♡ J 9 7 6 2          N               ♡ A Q 4
◇ 8 3             W     E             ◇ 10 5 2
♣ A 8 2              S               ♣ 10 9 6 5
                    ♠ Q 8 5 4
                    ♡ K 10 3
                    ◇ A Q 6
                    ♣ K J 4
```

Note the different considerations again. On Hand 1, East has the defensive entries so he plays the queen in an effort to keep communications intact.

In Hand 2, East has no entries, so he plays the ace and queen to clear up the position for West. If West has no fast entry, the 3 NT contract isn't going set.

The AQx combination discussed above is a common one and is very useful when handled correctly.

On very rare occasions, the same thing can be done with the AJx combination.

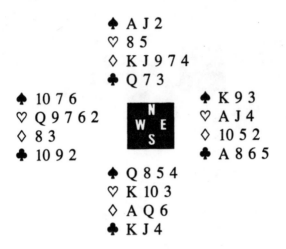

```
                    ♠ A J 2
                    ♡ 8 5
                    ◇ K J 9 7 4
                    ♣ Q 7 3
    ♠ 10 7 6                         ♠ K 9 3
    ♡ Q 9 7 6 2         N            ♡ A J 4
    ◇ 8 3          W    E            ◇ 10 5 2
    ♣ 10 9 2            S            ♣ A 8 6 5
                    ♠ Q 8 5 4
                    ♡ K 10 3
                    ◇ A Q 6
                    ♣ K J 4
```

If the auction were as before, 1 NT - Pass - 3 NT, then East could play the ♡J at trick one. Declarer would have to take the trick since AQxx in West's hand is a distinct danger. The reason it's so dangerous for East to play the jack is that West might have led from K10xxx. You would not like losing the jack to declarer's Qx if the suit were actually running.

The only time you would try the jack from AJx is when you know partner can't have the king, which is the case in the above hand.

Or, you might play the jack if you knew it would defeat the contract for sure.

North - South vulnerable — South deals

```
              ♠ A J 2
              ♡ 9 3
              ◇ A J 10 9 5
              ♣ Q 10 4
                          ♠ 9 8 5
                  N       ♡ A J 5
              W       E   ◇ K 6 4 2
                  S       ♣ A 5 3
```

West	North	East	South
			1♣
Pass	1◇	Pass	2♣
Pass	2♠	Pass	2 NT
Pass	3 NT	Pass	Pass
Pass			

Partner leads the ♡6. From your point of view, it doesn't matter if partner has K10xxx or Q10xxx.

If you play the jack, declarer will win and play on clubs or diamonds. You will win something and play ace and another heart. If declarer has KQx, it's just unlucky.

At matchpoints, you have an extremely difficult decision since the contract could be perfectly normal.

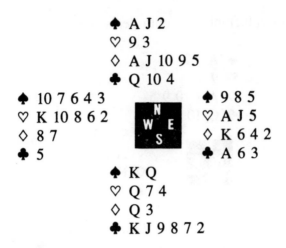

```
                    ♠ A J 2
                    ♡ 9 3
                    ◊ A J 10 9 5
                    ♣ Q 10 4
    ♠ 10 7 6 4 3              ♠ 9 8 5
    ♡ K 10 8 6 2              ♡ A J 5
    ◊ 8 7                     ◊ K 6 4 2
    ♣ 5                       ♣ A 6 3
                    ♠ K Q
                    ♡ Q 7 4
                    ◊ Q 3
                    ♣ K J 9 8 7 2
```

If this is the hand, playing the ♡J will cost a trick. You will still beat 3 NT by one trick, but the rest of the field will be beating it three tricks since your partner would win five heart tricks and then switch to a diamond.

At rubber bridge, or at IMPs, the ♡J would be correct.

Can you tell what you should do at matchpoints?

Not really. What is important is that you envision the possibilities and judge the approximate odds of one play as compared to another.

An extension of this suit combination looks like this:

No one vulnerable — West deals.

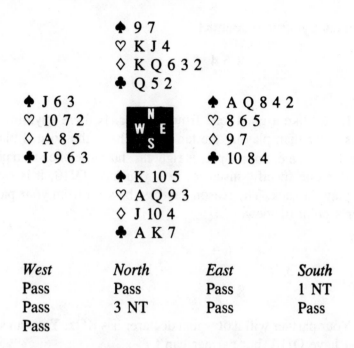

♠ 9 7
♡ K J 4
◊ K Q 6 3 2
♣ Q 5 2

♠ J 6 3
♡ 10 7 2
◊ A 8 5
♣ J 9 6 3

♠ A Q 8 4 2
♡ 8 6 5
◊ 9 7
♣ 10 8 4

♠ K 10 5
♡ A Q 9 3
◊ J 10 4
♣ A K 7

West	North	East	South
Pass	Pass	Pass	1 NT
Pass	3 NT	Pass	Pass
Pass			

West with no outstanding lead, led or guessed to lead, the
♠ 3. If East plays the ace and returns the suit, South will hold
up and will eventually take ten tricks.

If East plays the queen, the defense can prevail. Declarer
will take the king and the defense will now be able to take the
◊ A and four spade tricks.

The problem with this is that West won't always realize
what is going on and he may duck a diamond or two.

I have no solution for this problem. The defensive considerations are real though, so they are worth looking at, even if only
in theory.

Third Hand Falsecards to Help Partner

There are times when third hand must falsecard in order to
help the opening leader.

This sounds like a contradiction, to be sure. Nonetheless.

Versus a notrump contract.

```
            8 6 4
               *
  3                        Q J 10      ?
  *
```

Looks like a good lead from partner. Is there anything to this other than playing the ten spot? That's the normal play, and believe me, normal play is right far, far more often than not. In this one specific instance, i.e., you have QJ10, it is right to play the jack. The reason can best be seen from your partner's point of view.

```
            8 6 4
               *
  A 9 7 3                    10
     *                        *
          K
          *
```

Your partner will worry that declarer has KQx. You can see you have QJ10, but partner can't.

If you play the jack instead, this is what partner will see.

```
            8 6 4
               *
  A 9 7 3                    J
     *                        *
          K
          *
```

In this version, your partner will think one of two things:

1. You have the queen and it's right to lead low.
2. Declarer has the queen. But, because of your falsecard, partner will also think declarer has the ten. Therefore, from partner's point of view, it won't cost to lead low again since if declarer has KQ10, he has a sure stopper anyway.

Another falsecard intended to help partner is where you appear to be weak in a particular suit. The idea is to get partner to switch to something more rewarding.

Both vulnerable — North deals

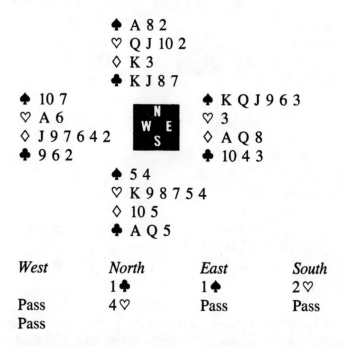

♠ A 8 2
♡ Q J 10 2
◇ K 3
♣ K J 8 7

♠ 10 7		♠ K Q J 9 6 3
♡ A 6		♡ 3
◇ J 9 7 6 4 2		◇ A Q 8
♣ 9 6 2		♣ 10 4 3

♠ 5 4
♡ K 9 8 7 5 4
◇ 10 5
♣ A Q 5

West	*North*	*East*	*South*
	1♣	1♠	2♡
Pass	4♡	Pass	Pass
Pass			

West leads the ♠10 to dummy's ace. What should East play?

East has a choice of plays. He might play the king as a suit preference, or he might play the three, which is not at all suit preference. The three would be interpreted as discouraging, and asking West to shift to something else.

Both the king and the three would be thinking plays.

What East should not do is play an encouraging nine. East does not want spades led. He wants diamonds.

By changing a card or two, we get this hand.

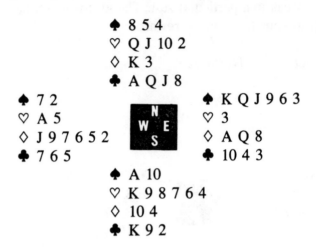

```
              ♠ 8 5 4
              ♡ Q J 10 2
              ◊ K 3
              ♣ A Q J 8
♠ 7 2                        ♠ K Q J 9 6 3
♡ A 5                        ♡ 3
◊ J 9 7 6 5 2                ◊ A Q 8
♣ 7 6 5                      ♣ 10 4 3
              ♠ A 10
              ♡ K 9 8 7 6 4
              ◊ 10 4
              ♣ K 9 2
```

The same auction.

West	North	East	South
	1♣	1♠	2♡
Pass	4♡	Pass	Pass
Pass			

West leads the ♠7 and East is in the same general position as before, i.e., he wants a diamond switch. The way East gets this across is by playing the ♠K. This creates the impression that declarer has the AQ and makes clear to West that there are no immediate spade tricks to be cashed. With luck, a thinking West will switch to the obvious suit, diamonds.

A falsecard which looks like the above, but which is made for a totally different purpose, is this one.

East - West vulnerable — North deals

```
                    ♠ K Q 10 7
                    ♡ 8 6 4
                    ◇ K 3
                    ♣ A Q 10 5
   ♠ 8 5 2                           ♠ A 9 3
   ♡ 10 7 5 2          N             ♡ K Q J
   ◇ A 4           W       E         ◇ 9 8 7 5
   ♣ 9 8 6 2          S             ♣ 7 4 3
                    ♠ J 6 4
                    ♡ A 9 3
                    ◇ Q J 10 6 2
                    ♣ K J
```

West	North	East	South
	1 ♣	Pass	1 ◇
Pass	1 ♠	Pass	2 NT
Pass	3 NT	Pass	Pass
Pass			

West leads the ♡2. How should the defense proceed?

What will probably happen is that declarer will hold up until the third round in hope that the hand with four hearts does not have an entry.

As you can see, that doesn't work on this hand.

It is possible for declarer to make this hand if he guesses to take the first or second heart and knocks out the ◇ A. With the hearts blocked, the defense will be shut out of their thirteenth heart.

How can declarer guess that the hearts are blocked? He can guess this is so if East tells him the hearts are blocked. If East plays the jack at trick one and continues with the king, declarer may visualize the actual holding.

The way East avoids this is to do one of several things. At trick one, he plays the jack as before, but at trick two, returns the queen, trying to look like a man with the ♡QJx, rather than the actual KQJ. Alternatively, East can play the queen and then the king, or he can play the king and then the jack.

East can tell declarer has the ♡A from the auction and he knows declarer will probably hold up twice. Therefore, the one thing East must not do is to give the show away by playing jack and then king.

If it turns out your partner has the ace, he may be momentarily surprised at what you are doing, but in the end, it will all be okay.

Sometimes your play in third hand is solely directed at stealing. Pure and simply larceny.

Both vulnerable — North deals

```
              ♠ 8 6 2
              ♡ A Q 9 6
              ◇ K 7 6 2
              ♣ Q 4
♠ J 9 5 3                      ♠ A K 7
♡ 4            N               ♡ 8 5 2
◇ J 9 8 5 3   W   E            ◇ Q 10
♣ A 9 3          S            ♣ 10 7 6 5 2
              ♠ Q 10 4
              ♡ K J 10 7 3
              ◇ A 4
              ♣ K J 8
```

West	North	East	South
	Pass	Pass	1 ♡
Pass	3 ♡	Pass	4 ♡
Pass	Pass	Pass	

West leads the ♠3 which East wins. This is a fairly standard situation which comes up frequently. East can tell the spades are 4-3-3-3 from West's lead. If West has the queen, the defense can take the first three tricks. But if West has the jack, the defense has only two tricks. Unless you can con a trick from an unsuspecting South.

If East wins the opening lead with the ace, and returns the seven, South may misguess and finesse the ten.

You may worry that this will cost a trick. It shouldn't. If declarer has QJx, it would leave your partner with 109xx and he might have led the ten. If declarer has Q9x or worse, that would leave your partner with J10xx and your partner might have led the jack from this holding. With the spots being as they are, you can underlead the king rather fearlessly. Either your partner has the queen or declarer has the Q10x which he will likely misguess.

Gotta watch those spots. If you lose one and it turns out partner has led from jack fifth . . . trouble!

Midgame Leads

Because the opening leader is often in the blind about the opponents' strength and distribution, there are restraints on what he can do. You would never, for instance, lead the king from KJ3, nor would you lead low from AK3, and you certainly wouldn't lead the ten of trump from 10864.

Once the dummy appears though, all bets are off and as certain facts become available, almost anything may be right.

There are times where you have the option of opening up a suit and there are times where declarer has endplayed you and you have to open up a suit. According to the urgency, you may have to try some pretty drastic maneuvers.

Q 10 4

8 7 3

This position looks rather dull. Declarer, sooner or later, will lead to the ten, hoping to find LHO with AJx or KJx. He could play LHO for AKx, but this is only half as likely as either AJx or KJx. If declarer has some compelling information though, it could be correct to lead to the queen.

```
                   Q 10 4
    K J 6 2                      A 9 5
                   8 7 3
```

In this position, it appears that declarer will get a trick eventually, unless declarer misguesses.

The key word here is "misguesses." Almost without exception, when there is a guess to be made, there is something the other side can do to make that guess more difficult.

For instance, there are three things West can do to confuse declarer in this position above.

1. West can lead the king and then small. Declarer may opt to play the queen. This actually should not work, but it may. The reason it should not work is that if West started with AKx, he might have been tempted to lead the suit on opening lead, OR, he might have chosen to underlead the AKx rather than to play king and then low.

2. If West wants to take a chance that his partner has the nine spot, he can lead the jack. It will go to the queen and ace. Now if West gets in again, he can underlead the king a second time. Declarer might duck this to East's nine.

3. West might lead the two or the six. The reason this can work is that this is how a good defender might play if he did, in fact, have AKx. It's not all that often that a defender leads through the Q10x in dummy and declarer may be fooled simply because the defense is leading the suit at all.

```
            Q 10 4
  A K 9 5                    J 6 2
            8 7 3
```

If declarer plays the suit himself, he will usually misguess unless the defense gives the show away. West himself may lead the suit (trick two or later) before declarer does and if he leads the five, he rates to steal a trick almost all of the time.

Once a declarer has been burned a couple of times with this swindle, he will be ripe for a defender who leads the six from KJ62 (see previous diagram).

On a theoretical level, West might even lead the K from AKx before leading low. In fact, against an expert declarer, this could work.

```
            J 5 2
  Q 10 7                     K 8 6 4
            A 9 3
```

East in this diagram, if he chooses to lead the suit at all, should lead the king. If declarer believes this lead to be from KQ10, he will duck. This will lead to two or three tricks for the defense. There are two reasons East may do this. He may have been the victim of an endplay in which case he is trying to get two tricks. Or he may be defending a notrump contract and has concluded that three tricks are necessary in this suit.

East - West vulnerable — South deals

```
                    ♠ Q 10 9 4 2
                    ♡ J 9 3
                    ◇ A J 4
                    ♣ K 5
    ♠ 8 6                              ♠ A K 5 3
    ♡ Q 10 2         N                ♡ K 7 6 5
    ◇ 10 9 8 3     W   E              ◇ Q 6 5
    ♣ J 9 7 3         S                ♣ 10 4
                    ♠ J 7
                    ♡ A 8 4
                    ◇ K 7 2
                    ♣ A Q 8 6 2
```

West	North	East	South
			1 ♣
Pass	1 ♠	Pass	1 NT
Pass	2 NT	Pass	3 NT
Pass	Pass	Pass	

West leads the ◇ 10 to the jack, queen and king. The ♠ J
goes to East's king.

East can appreciate two things.

1. Even if diamonds can be established, West won't have an
    entry.
2. West is unlikely to have more than a queen.

Appreciating that the defense will have to set up heart tricks,
East switches to the ♡ K. Declarer can make his contract by
taking either the ♡ K or the second heart, but the odds are
heavily in favor of the falsecard working.

If the defense is desperate, it can try this variation.

                    J 9 3
K 10 4 2   Q 7 5
    ★   A 8 6

This really shouldn't work, but it could.

                    J 9 3
K Q 4 2   10 8 5
    ★   A 7 6

This one has excellent chances of being successful.

                    Q 5 2
A J 7   10 6 4 3
    ★   K 9 8

If West has been endplayed, or if time is short, the jack is the
right card here. Declarer will let this come to his king. Eventually, West will underlead the ace again.

                    Q 5 2
A J 7   K 9 8 4
    ★   10 6 3

Leading the jack is not always done as a falsecard. In this combination, the jack must be led to keep declarer from getting
a trick.

                    Q 6 4
J 7 2   A 10 5 3
    ★   K 9 8

Another variation on this combination. When the jack is led,
declarer has to guess if West has:

AJx, Jxx or J10x.

All of these holdings are possible. Bridge is not always an easy game. Positions like these bring a certain spark to otherwise dull hands. As my guru once told me . . . Go Guess!

```
                    K 8 2
      A Q 5                      J 9 6 4
        *           10 7 3
```

This lead, unlike the others in this section, was looked at in the discussion on opening leads. The idea was to induce declarer to duck the queen, and then the five to East's jack. There is another sound reason for this play other than deception. Say the suit is slightly different, and say that West has been endplayed so that he must open up this suit.

```
                    K 9 2
      A Q 5                      10 8 4 3
        *           J 7 6
```

If West leads the ace or the five, declarer will get two tricks. If West leads the queen, the king will win, but declarer will still remain with two losers.

If Truly Endplayed

```
                    A 10 6 2
      Q 7 5                      J 8 3
        *           K 9 4        *
```

There are some plays you would prefer not to have to make. At times they become unavoidable and you have to make do. In this setting, if either defender is obliged to lead this suit, he should lead his honor. If you lead low in this position, declarer will be forced to play for split honors.

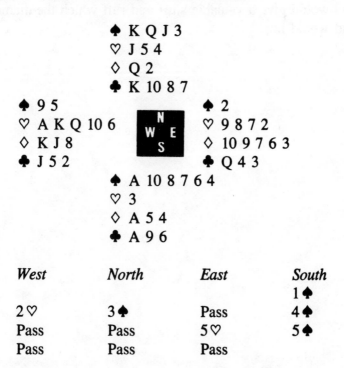

K 9 8

10 6 3   A J 7 2

Q 5 4

This position is almost the same as was discussed two pages ago. If East is forced to lead this suit, he should lead the jack and hope declarer misguesses. This position comes up more often than you might think, certainly more often than you like. So it's an important position to recognize.

When you think you have been endplayed, you should make sure it has really happened and that you haven't just been pseudo endplayed.

North - South vulnerable — South deals

                        ♠ K Q J 3
                        ♡ J 5 4
                        ◊ Q 2
                        ♣ K 10 8 7
    ♠ 9 5   ♠ 2
    ♡ A K Q 10 6   N   ♡ 9 8 7 2
    ◊ K J 8   W   E   ◊ 10 9 7 6 3
    ♣ J 5 2   S   ♣ Q 4 3
                        ♠ A 10 8 7 6 4
                        ♡ 3
                        ◊ A 5 4
                        ♣ A 9 6

West	North	East	South
			1 ♠
2 ♡	3 ♠	Pass	4 ♠
Pass	Pass	5 ♡	5 ♠
Pass	Pass	Pass	

East's unorthodox approach has pushed South to 5 ♠. Against this contract, West leads the two top hearts and South ruffs the second round. South plays the ♠ AK, and ruffs dummy's last heart. Ace and a diamond puts West on play.

If West thinks he is truly endplayed, he should lead the ♣ J, and this is what would happen frequently. West should see that this endplay is not complete. West knows declarer has six spades, one heart and at least two diamonds. If East-West were giving count signals, declarer's hand would have no mysteries at all. But even without these signals, the defense should succeed.

From West's point of view, if declarer has four clubs so that a diamond gives a sluff and a ruff, it won't hurt the defense since declarer will still have a club loser. West must be careful to lead a diamond and not a heart in this position, since, if declarer did have only three clubs plus three diamonds, the heart lead would give a valuable sluff and ruff which the diamond lead would not.

Chapter 3

FALSECARDS IN AND AROUND
THE TRUMP SUIT

Threatening a Ruff That Isn't There

Often, when defending against a suit contract, the only way to defeat a contract is by getting a ruff.

Declarer is well aware of that and his line of play must take defensive ruffs into consideration. Naturally, one of the techniques available to declarer is drawing trumps.

Sometimes when the defense threatens to get a ruff, declarer will respond by drawing trumps with excess urgency.

For example:

North - South vulnerable — North deals.

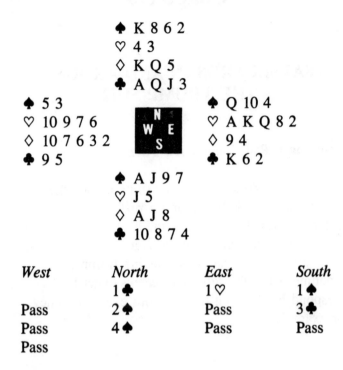

	♠ K 8 6 2	
	♡ 4 3	
	◊ K Q 5	
	♣ A Q J 3	

West	North	East	South
	1♣	1♡	1♠
Pass	2♠	Pass	3♣
Pass	4♠	Pass	Pass
Pass			

West leads the ♡10 and East takes the queen and ace. If West has the ♠J, the contract will be set routinely, but if declarer's spades are headed by the AJ, then there is little or no chance, unless declarer can be talked out of the trump finesse.

East can give declarer something to worry about by returning the ♣6. He knows from the auction that his club trick will still be available. If declarer can be talked out of the trump finesse, for fear of a club ruff, the defense may get a club and a spade trick.

A little more likely to come up is a hand like the following.

No one vulnerable — South deals

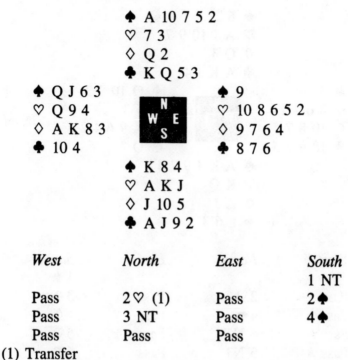

	♠ A 10 7 5 2	
	♡ 7 3	
	◇ Q 2	
	♣ K Q 5 3	

♠ Q J 6 3		♠ 9
♡ Q 9 4		♡ 10 8 6 5 2
◇ A K 8 3		◇ 9 7 6 4
♣ 10 4		♣ 8 7 6

	♠ K 8 4	
	♡ A K J	
	◇ J 10 5	
	♣ A J 9 2	

West	North	East	South
			1 NT
Pass	2♡ (1)	Pass	2♠
Pass	3 NT	Pass	4♠
Pass	Pass	Pass	

(1) Transfer

West leads the ◇ K and ◇ A. In order to discourage declarer from taking a safety play in spades, West shifts to the ♣4. This threatens a club ruff so South may play the ♠K and ♠A to shut off a ruff. There will be no ruff, but the contract will still fail.

It's possible that this falsecard can be used at trick one as well.

Both vulnerable — South deals

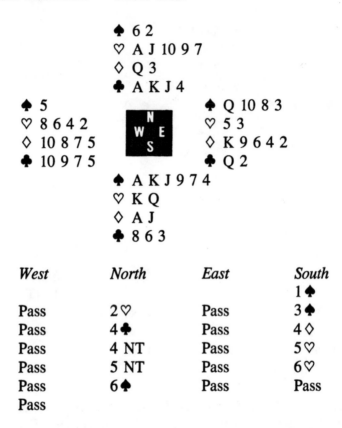

	♠ 6 2		
	♡ A J 10 9 7		
	◇ Q 3		
	♣ A K J 4		

	North		
♠ 5		♠ Q 10 8 3
♡ 8 6 4 2		♡ 5 3
◇ 10 8 7 5		◇ K 9 6 4 2
♣ 10 9 7 5		♣ Q 2

	♠ A K J 9 7 4		
	♡ K Q		
	◇ A J		
	♣ 8 6 3		

West	North	East	South
			1 ♠
Pass	2 ♡	Pass	3 ♠
Pass	4 ♣	Pass	4 ◇
Pass	4 NT	Pass	5 ♡
Pass	5 NT	Pass	6 ♡
Pass	6 ♠	Pass	Pass
Pass			

West leads the ♣ 10 and East drops the queen. I'll bet declarer takes no spade finesse.

Camouflaging Whether a Defender Can Ruff — Faking an Uppercut

The falsecard has many forms. You may wish to pretend your side can ruff or you may pretend your side can't ruff.

One treasured weapon for the defense is the uppercut. It works in two basic ways.

```
          x x x x
Q x                       J x
          A K x x x
```

This is trumps and it appears declarer has no losers. If the defense can lead a suit such that East ruffs with the jack, declarer will lose a trick if he overruffs and, of course, loses the immediate trick if he doesn't.

The second way is, using the same diagram, if East leads a suit that South and West are void in. If South ruffs high, the defense gets a later trump trick.

Sometimes the defense can persuade declarer a ruff is coming when in fact it isn't. Declarer may ruff high and then find out it was unnecessary and expensive.

East - West vulnerable — East deals

```
                    ♠ J 7 2
                    ♡ Q 8 2
                    ◇ K Q
                    ♣ J 7 6 4 2
     ♠ 6 5 4              ♠ A K 10 8 3
     ♡ J 9 5        N     ♡ —
     ◇ 10 7 3 2   W   E   ◇ A 9 6 4
     ♣ K 10 9       S     ♣ Q 8 5 3
                    ♠ Q 9
                    ♡ A K 10 7 6 4 3
                    ◇ J 8 5
                    ♣ A
```

West	North	East	South
		1 ♠	2 ♡
Pass	3 ♡	Pass	4 ♡
Pass	Pass	Pass	

93

West leads the ♠6. East takes the ♠A and ♠K, the ◊A and leads another spade. If West plays his spade with no evident problem, i.e., in tempo, declarer may fear a ruff and will ruff high himself. The ♡J95 will be the setting trick.

East - West vulnerable — South deals

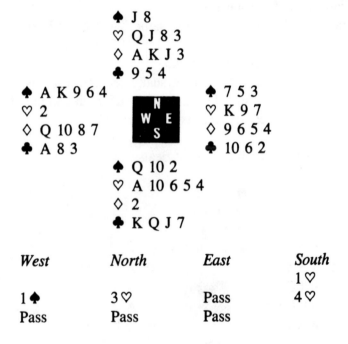

	♠ J 8	
	♡ Q J 8 3	
	◊ A K J 3	
	♣ 9 5 4	
♠ A K 9 6 4		♠ 7 5 3
♡ 2		♡ K 9 7
◊ Q 10 8 7		◊ 9 6 5 4
♣ A 8 3		♣ 10 6 2
	♠ Q 10 2	
	♡ A 10 6 5 4	
	◊ 2	
	♣ K Q J 7	

West	North	East	South
			1 ♡
1 ♠	3 ♡	Pass	4 ♡
Pass	Pass	Pass	

West leads the ♠K and ♠A. East sees that if dummy can be tricked into ruffing the third spade with an honor, he will get a trump trick. East therefore echos in spades with the 7-3. This will likely fool everyone. West will lead a third spade and declarer probably will fall for it by ruffing high in dummy.

East - West vulnerable — North deals

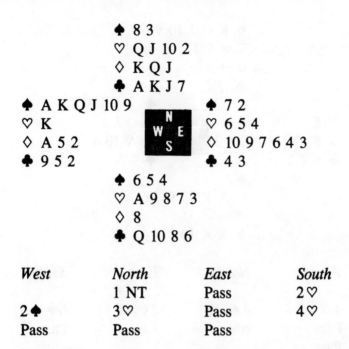

♠ 8 3
♡ Q J 10 2
◇ K Q J
♣ A K J 7

♠ A K Q J 10 9
♡ K
◇ A 5 2
♣ 9 5 2

♠ 7 2
♡ 6 5 4
◇ 10 9 7 6 4 3
♣ 4 3

♠ 6 5 4
♡ A 9 8 7 3
◇ 8
♣ Q 10 8 6

West	North	East	South
	1 NT	Pass	2♡
2♠	3♡	Pass	4♡
Pass	Pass	Pass	

West leads the ♠K and East plays the seven. West can tell it's a singleton or doubleton, but does not continue spades because he knows East can't overruff dummy. West first switches to the ♣9. Declarer has no clear reason not to finesse the heart and does so. West now can take the setting tricks.

Had West played three rounds of spades, the heart position would have become known and declarer would have tried to drop the ♡K. In this case, successfully.

The following hand is a more elegant example of hiding partner's exact trump holding.

East - West vulnerable — South deals

```
                    ♠ K Q J 10 9 6
                    ♡ 8 4 2
                    ◇ 9 3
                    ♣ Q J
    ♠ 7                             ♠ A 5 4 3 2
    ♡ 5                    N         ♡ Q J 3
    ◇ K Q J 8 7 6 5 2   W   E       ◇ A 10 4
    ♣ 6 4 2                S         ♣ 7 5
                    ♠ 8
                    ♡ A K 10 9 7 6
                    ◇ —
                    ♣ A K 10 9 8 3
```

West	North	East	South
			1 ♡
4 ◇	4 ♠	5 ◇	6 ♣
Pass	6 ♡	Pass	Pass
Pass			

Note East's final pass. An excellent decision. Double might gain 50 points but it risks telling declarer how to play the hand.

West correctly guessed there were no diamond tricks and led his stiff spade. When East won, he was able to reconstruct the hand completely.

Since West had led a stiff spade, he had to have at least one trump so declarer has a maximum of six hearts. West's 4 ◇ bid on this vulnerability ought to show eight diamonds, so declarer is void. Declarer, therefore, must have six hearts and six clubs, both suits headed by the ace-king.

If East returns a spade, declarer will ruff with some spot card and when West can't overruff, declarer will pick up the trump suit by finessing against the QJ.

Better is for East to try to cash the ◇ A. This play won't

look too suspicious and declarer will have less reason to play the hearts correctly.

It's true that if West has the singleton ♡9, a spade return will set 6♡ via an uppercut. I think, though, that weighing the possibilities should lead to the falsecard play of the ◊A.

A rather uncommon strategy is to make a play which seems to suggest that your partner is not ruffing, when he really is.

Both vulnerable — East deals

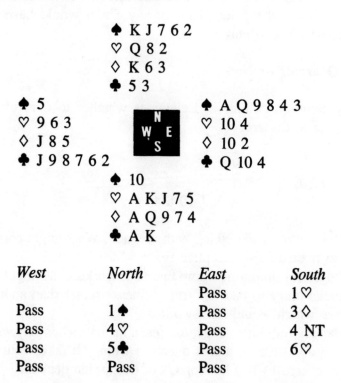

```
                    ♠ K J 7 6 2
                    ♡ Q 8 2
                    ◊ K 6 3
                    ♣ 5 3
    ♠ 5                            ♠ A Q 9 8 4 3
    ♡ 9 6 3              N         ♡ 10 4
    ◊ J 8 5          W     E       ◊ 10 2
    ♣ J 9 8 7 6 2       S         ♣ Q 10 4
                    ♠ 10
                    ♡ A K J 7 5
                    ◊ A Q 9 7 4
                    ♣ A K
```

West	North	East	South
		Pass	1 ♡
Pass	1 ♠	Pass	3 ◊
Pass	4 ♡	Pass	4 NT
Pass	5 ♣	Pass	6 ♡
Pass	Pass	Pass	

West leads his stiff spade. East wins with the Ace! and returns a spade. Declarer may pitch a diamond rather than ruff high. Down one. If East had won the queen and returned a small spade, declarer might have smelled a rat and ruffed high.

There's one falsecard I've been waiting for, for years. It requires a specific card combination which probably explains its rarity.

```
                    A J 9 2
     10 8 6 4                      Q
                    K 7 5 3
```

If West decides he should lead this suit (trick two or later), he should lead the ten. I doubt any South would have the awareness not to play the jack.

To Overruff or Not

A common defensive decision is whether to overruff or whether to discard.

```
                    9 3
     Q 7 6                        5 2
                    A K J 10 8 4
```

If declarer ruffs something with the jack, West might choose not to overruff for deceptive reasons.

If declarer thinks the trump finesse is working, he might use a crucial entry to take the trump finesse rather than another finesse which would have worked.

There is very little danger to West if he makes this play when holding Qx or even a stiff queen of trump. It takes courage not to overruff when holding Qx of trump, but declarer is not likely to guess the situation. Would you?

Another, more significant reason for not overruffing is not that you are fooling declarer, but that you are gaining a trick via an uppercut.

Sometimes the trick you gain is immediately visible.

```
                7 6 4 2
A J                                        5
                K Q 10 9 8 3
```

Declarer usually loses only one trick in this setting. But, if declarer is forced to ruff with the king or queen, West gains a trick by not overruffing.

```
                8 6 2
K 10 5                                  7 4
                A Q J 9 3
```

Likewise, West should not overruff if declarer ruffs with the queen or jack.

```
                8 6 2
K 9 4                                  10 7
                A Q J 5 3
```

If declarer ruffs with the queen, West should not overruff. East has the ten, which means West's nine becomes a winner if he waits.

Some trump promotions aren't so obvious.

East - West vulnerable — South deals

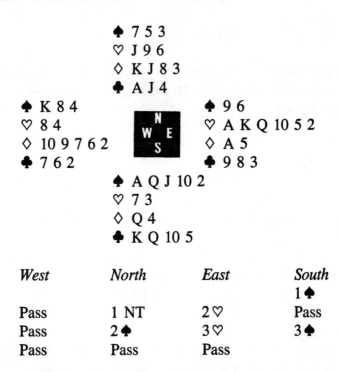

	♠ 7 5 3	
	♡ J 9 6	
	◊ K J 8 3	
	♣ A J 4	

```
              ♠ 7 5 3
              ♡ J 9 6
              ◊ K J 8 3
              ♣ A J 4
  ♠ K 8 4                    ♠ 9 6
  ♡ 8 4           N          ♡ A K Q 10 5 2
  ◊ 10 9 7 6 2  W   E        ◊ A 5
  ♣ 7 6 2         S          ♣ 9 8 3
              ♠ A Q J 10 2
              ♡ 7 3
              ◊ Q 4
              ♣ K Q 10 5
```

West	North	East	South
			1♠
Pass	1 NT	2♡	Pass
Pass	2♣	3♡	3♠
Pass	Pass	Pass	

West leads hearts and East plays three rounds. Declarer ruffs with the queen and West, with no reason to overruff, discards a club. Declarer enters dummy with a club and finesses the ♠J. West wins this one, puts East in with a diamond, and now the fourth round of hearts produces the setting trick from the ♠8.

```
        7 3
Q 9                 A 6 4
        K J 10 8 5 2
```

If, at an early stage, declarer ruffs with the jack and West overruffs, declarer will lose one additional trump trick. If West refuses to overruff, declarer may later finesse the ten into West's queen. Then, with luck, South will next finesse the eight, losing to the nine. Ergo, three trump losers.

There are many positions where overruffing is wrong both from a technical and deceptive point of view.

```
                    10 3
    7 6                             Q 9 5 4
                    A K J 8 2
```

If South ruffs something with dummy's ten, East does best not to overruff. Declarer may get the idea that West has the queen of trump and try to drop it.

```
                    K 10
    Q 2                             J 8 4 3
                    A 9 7 6 5
```

If declarer ruffs with the ten and East overruffs, that's the last trick for the defense. If East refuses to overruff, the defense gets two tricks.

```
                    Q J 3
    10 5                            K 9 7
                    A 8 6 4 2
```

Again, if declarer ruffs with the queen the defense gains a trick by not overruffing.

```
                    7 5
    J 6 3 2                         Q 8
                    A K 10 9 4
```

If South ruffs with the ten, West comes to two tricks if he shows patience.

10
9 6 4 2   Q J
A K 8 7 5 3

With the 9642 of trump, you might not have expected even one trick, yet if declarer is forced to ruff with the seven, West can get two tricks out of this by refusing to overruff.

Chapter 4

PLAYING THE CARD
YOU ARE KNOWN TO HOLD

When you are declaring a hand, you will have constant decisions to make. Two of the factors you must consider are the opponents' high cards and the opponents' distribution. As a defender, it is in your interest to confuse the issue as much as possible without confusing partner.

PLAYING THE CARD YOU ARE KNOWN TO HOLD means just that. Often you will have a choice of cards to play. If you are known to have a certain card and if you can afford to play it, you usually should do so.

```
              A 9 4 2
  8 7 6                   Q 10 5
              K J 3
```

Declarer finesses the jack and plays the king. If East holds onto his queen, declarer won't be hard pressed to go up with the ace on the third round.

If East drops the queen (the card he is known to hold) on the king, declarer has a genuine guess and may finesse the nine.

```
              K 8 6 2
  A 7 5                   J 9 3
              Q 10 4
```

After declarer finesses the ten to the ace, East must drop the jack when declarer plays the queen.

East - West vulnerable — South deals.

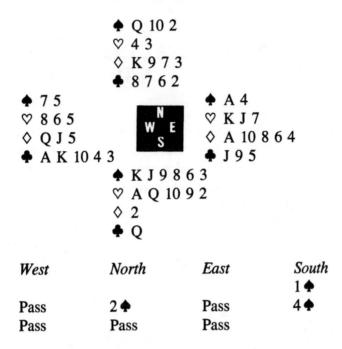

	♠ Q 10 2	
	♡ 4 3	
	◊ K 9 7 3	
	♣ 8 7 6 2	

♠ 7 5   ♠ A 4
♡ 8 6 5   ♡ K J 7
◊ Q J 5   ◊ A 10 8 6 4
♣ A K 10 4 3   ♣ J 9 5

♠ K J 9 8 6 3
♡ A Q 10 9 2
◊ 2
♣ Q

West	North	East	South
			1♠
Pass	2♠	Pass	4♠
Pass	Pass	Pass	

West started with two top clubs and South ruffed. A spade to the queen went to East's ace. South ruffed the next club and drew trumps with dummy's ♠ 10. A heart to the queen was followed by the ace. If East has followed routinely with the seven and jack, declarer will ruff a heart for ten tricks. If East follows with the seven and king, declarer may lead the ♡ 10 and finesse it to East's jack.

These falsecards are as close as any falsecards are to being mandatory. Your partner can usually tell what is happening so there is not much to lose from fooling partner. But much is gained when declarer isn't given a free rein. Any time you can give declarer an option, you have the chance that declarer will do something wrong.

```
              4 2
10 8 6 3                    A Q 5
              K J 9 7
```

If declarer leads to his king, East should win the next trick with the ace rather than the queen.

```
              A Q 7 2
K J 9 5                    10 6 4
              8 3
```

If declarer finesses the queen and then plays the ace, West should drop the king. Declarer may not realize he can ruff back to his hand in this suit. If he fears an overruff, he may concoct some way to lose a trick where no loser exists.

```
              A Q 10 6 2
K J 9 7                    8
              5 4 3
```

Declarer finesses the ten which wins. When declarer repeats the finesse, West must play the jack. If declarer finesses the queen, he will get three tricks, but will not get four unless he has an extra entry to dummy. If West plays the nine on the second round, Declarer may work out the suit is 4-1 and can duck the trick completely, thus maintaining communcations.

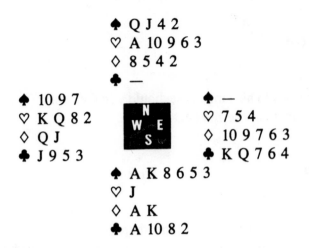

♠ Q J 4 2
♡ A 10 9 6 3
♢ 8 5 4 2
♣ —

♠ 10 9 7
♡ K Q 8 2
♢ Q J
♣ J 9 5 3

♠ —
♡ 7 5 4
♢ 10 9 7 6 3
♣ K Q 7 6 4

♠ A K 8 6 5 3
♡ J
♢ A K
♣ A 10 8 2

Against 7♠, West leads the ♡K. Declarer wins and cashes the ♠Q, noting the bad break. The play continues:

3.   ♢A
4.   Club ruff
5.   ♢K
6.   Club ruff
7.   Heart ruff — West drops the card he is known to hold — the ♡Q.
8.   Club ruff
9.   Declarer can get to his hand with a heart ruff. But he doesn't know it. He will probably try to ruff a diamond instead.

Chapter 5

MORE MANDATORY FALSECARDS

Continuing in the family of mandatory falsecards is the following situation as seen by declarer.

```
              6
              ♣
   5                        3
   ♣                        ♣
         K Q 9 8 7 4 2
              ♣
```

Declarer leads the six to his king. When West plays the five, declarer has only one option and that is to lead the two, hoping East started life with the A3 doubleton.

```
              6
              ♣
   J                        3
   ♣                        ♣
         K Q 9 8 7 4 2
              ♣
```

If West follows with the jack, declarer can still play East for the A3 doubleton. But he also has the added option of leading the queen, hoping for J10 doubleton in West's hand.

Since declarer has two possible plays, there is a measurable chance that he will sometimes make the wrong play.

There are many opportunities for a defender to misrepresent his holding to appear as something it isn't.

```
                6
                ★
    J 10 5                          A 3
      *                               *
                K Q 9 8 7 4 2
                *
    ─────────────────────────────────
                6
    J 10                            A 5 3
                K Q 9 8 7 4 2
```

This is the combination just discussed. West drops the ten, making it appear that he has the J10 doubleton as in the second diagram. If declarer tries the queen, the defense gains a trick.

In the following diagrams, the defense plays the first combination, hoping declarer will play for the second combination.

```
                6 2
                ★
    J 10 5                          A 3
      *                               *
                K Q 9 8 7 4
                *
    ─────────────────────────────────
                6 2
    J 10                            A 5 3
                K Q 9 8 7 4
```

This combination is the same as the previous one, except that dummy has one of declarer's small cards. If, however, dummy has no reentry, the defense is still obliged to find the falsecard.

                          —
J 10 8 2   K 3
            A Q 9 7 6 5 4

                          —
J 8   K 10 3 2
            A Q 9 7 6 5 4

If declarer thinks the second diagram exists, his proper continution is the queen.

                          —
10 9 8 3   Q 5 2
            A K J 7 6 4

                          —
10 9 8   Q 5 3 2
            A K J 7 6 4

Again, declarer may decide the jack is his best play now. Certainly, it is if the second hand diagram exists.

Chapter 6

ENTRY-CREATING FALSECARDS

```
              Q 8 2
   5          ♣            7
   ♣                       ♣
              K 9 6 4 3
                ♣
```

When declarer leads the three to the queen, his best play for
only one loser is to lead to his hand, ducking whatever East
plays. If West started with A5 doubleton, declarer can run the
suit with only one loser.

Trading on declarer's intentions to play the suit in the above
manner, the defense can come up with some pretty swindles.

```
              Q 8 2
   J 5        ♣            A 10 7
   ♣                       ♣
              K 9 6 4 3
                ♣
```

When declarer ducks on the way back, West takes his jack.
If West is in need of an entry, this can be crucial to the defense.

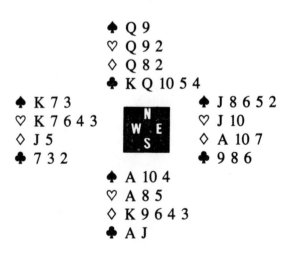

```
              ♠ Q 9
              ♡ Q 9 2
              ◊ Q 8 2
              ♣ K Q 10 5 4
♠ K 7 3                      ♠ J 8 6 5 2
♡ K 7 6 4 3        N         ♡ J 10
◊ J 5          W       E     ◊ A 10 7
♣ 7 3 2            S         ♣ 9 8 6
              ♠ A 10 4
              ♡ A 8 5
              ◊ K 9 6 4 3
              ♣ A J
```

How did South go down in 3 NT? Not easy, but it was reasonable. West led a heart to the ten and ace. The ◊ Q won and the diamond continuation went to West's jack. A second small heart went to East's jack as declarer reasonably misguessed the suit also. A spade return left declarer two down. Mercifully, the defense never did get its ◊ A.

This variation is also possible.

<pre>
              Q 8 2
              ♣
 10 5   A J 7
   ♣   ♣
              K 9 6 4 3
                  ♣
</pre>

When declarer next leads toward his king, East's jack will win unless declarer makes an inspired guess. This has the effect of giving East an extra entry.

It may look dangerous for East to duck with the AJ7, but it shouldn't be if he can duck smoothly. If declarer has K10xxx, he would finesse against East's jack, so there never was a second trick for East. Only if declarer has a six-card suit (K10xxxx) will East's play make a difference.

<pre>
              Q 8 2
              ♣
 J 10   A 7 6
   ♣   ♣
              K 9 5 4 3
                  ♣
</pre>

In this similar combination, East ducks as a point of technique. If East takes the ace, declarer is likely to drop the jack rather than to finesse. East's duck pretty much ensures that declarer will go wrong.

Chapter 7

ODD SITUATIONS

Not all falsecards fall conveniently into categories. Some stand more or less by themselves.

Misrepresenting Your Length in a Suit

Both vulnerable — West deals

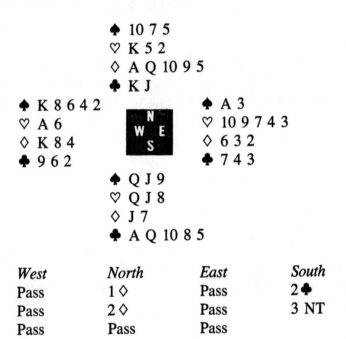

```
                ♠ 10 7 5
                ♡ K 5 2
                ◊ A Q 10 9 5
                ♣ K J
  ♠ K 8 6 4 2              ♠ A 3
  ♡ A 6                    ♡ 10 9 7 4 3
  ◊ K 8 4                  ◊ 6 3 2
  ♣ 9 6 2                  ♣ 7 4 3
                ♠ Q J 9
                ♡ Q J 8
                ◊ J 7
                ♣ A Q 10 8 5
```

West	North	East	South
Pass	1 ◊	Pass	2 ♣
Pass	2 ◊	Pass	3 NT
Pass	Pass	Pass	

West leads the ♠4 won by East's ace. When East returns the three, West has a choice of winning and clearing the suit, or ducking.

If West wins and establishes spades, declarer will see the 5-2 division. Declarer may decide it's too dangerous to set up

112

hearts and may choose to take the diamond finesse instead.

If West ducks the spade return, and falsecards with the six, declarer may play the spade suit to be 4-3, i.e., K864 opposite A32. If spades are 4-3, declarer can guarantee 3 NT by knocking out the ♡A.

Curiously, if West did not have the ◊K, he should play a third spade to show declarer the bad news. Now declarer might take the diamond finesse which leads to down two.

No one vulnerable — East deals.

```
                    ♠ A J 6 4
                    ♡ J 5
                    ◊ J 7 6 4 3
                    ♣ 9 5
  ♠ K Q 10 8                      ♠ 9 7 5 2
  ♡ Q 8 6 4 3 2        N          ♡ 9 7
  ◊ 10 2            W     E        ◊ K 5
  ♣ 8                  S          ♣ 10 6 4 3 2
                    ♠ 3
                    ♡ A K 10
                    ◊ A Q 9 8
                    ♣ A K Q J 7
```

West	North	East	South
		Pass	1 ♣
Pass	1 ♠	Pass	2 ◊
Pass	3 ◊	Pass	4 NT
Pass	5 ◊	Pass	7 ◊
Pass	Pass	Pass	

Not your ideal contract, but it was reached in the final of a National event.

Declarer won the ♠K lead in dummy and led the ◊3 to the queen. With the ◊K about to fall, it looked like 7 ◊ was going to be a lucky make.

When West followed with the ◊ 10, though, declarer suddenly had a new problem. It looked like East had three diamonds to the king so another finesse was necessary.

How would you try to get to dummy? By ruffing a heart or by ruffing a club? Declarer tried to ruff a heart and that didn't work. One down.

$$\begin{array}{ccc}
 & Q\ J\ 9\ 5 & \\
 & * & \\
7 & & A\ K\ 10\ 3\ 2 \\
* & & * \\
 & 8\ 6\ 4 & \\
 & ★ &
\end{array}$$

If declarer thinks this suit is breaking, he may come back and try it again.

$$\begin{array}{ccc}
 & K\ J\ 4 & \\
 & * & \\
10 & & A\ Q\ 9\ 7\ 2 \\
* & & * \\
 & 8\ 6\ 5\ 3 & \\
 & ★ &
\end{array}$$

Likewise.

$$\begin{array}{ccc}
 & K\ J\ 5 & \\
 & * & \\
6 & & A\ Q\ 8\ 7\ 3 \\
* & & * \\
 & 10\ 9\ 4\ 2 & \\
 & ★ &
\end{array}$$

If declarer leads this suit again, East can establish it to his benefit.

Pretending to be Out of a Suit

East - West vulnerable — East deals

```
                        ♠ A 10 9 2
                        ♡ Q J 5 4
                        ◇ A J 2
                        ♣ A 7
        ♠ 8 7 3                          ♠ K 6 5
        ♡ 9 3 2            N             ♡ 10 8 7 6
        ◇ 8 5 3        W       E         ◇ K 6 4
        ♣ K J 9 5          S             ♣ Q 10 3
                        ♠ Q J 4
                        ♡ A K
                        ◇ Q 10 9 7
                        ♣ 8 6 4 2
```

West	North	East	South
		Pass	1 ◇
Pass	1 ♡	Pass	1 NT
Pass	3 NT	Pass	Pass
Pass			

West led the ♣5 won by East's queen. The ♣10 was returned to the ace. Declarer came to his hand with a heart and finessed in spades to East's king.

Had East returned a club, the defense would have taken four tricks, but that would be the end of the defense.

Instead, East returned a spade trying to look like a defender with no more clubs. Declarer now has the option of taking a diamond finesse for a possible eleven tricks.

Should this falsecard succeed? Possibly. Possibly not. If declarer is playing matchpoints he may well go for the extra tricks and end up going down in a cold contract.

The following is a peculiar falsecard for which there is no good guideline. It may, in fact, seem unbelievable except for the fact that the auction and play went as described in a match between two excellent pairs.

North - South vulnerable — South deals

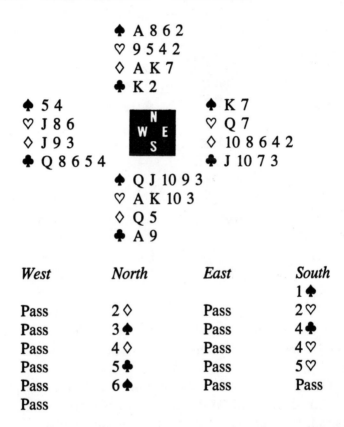

	♠ A 8 6 2		
	♡ 9 5 4 2		
	◊ A K 7		
	♣ K 2		

♠ 5 4		♠ K 7
♡ J 8 6		♡ Q 7
◊ J 9 3		◊ 10 8 6 4 2
♣ Q 8 6 5 4		♣ J 10 7 3

	♠ Q J 10 9 3
	♡ A K 10 3
	◊ Q 5
	♣ A 9

West	North	East	South
			1 ♠
Pass	2 ◊	Pass	2 ♡
Pass	3 ♠	Pass	4 ♣
Pass	4 ◊	Pass	4 ♡
Pass	5 ♣	Pass	5 ♡
Pass	6 ♠	Pass	Pass
Pass			

This is a very good slam which has chances even when the spade finesse loses. This time, however, 6 ♠ looks to be going down.

Declarer, somehow blessed with more than normal intuition, embarked on a double dummy line which was going to succeed.

Winning the club lead, declarer played in order:

1.   ♣ K
2.   ♦ Q
3.   ♦ A
4.   ♦ K, pitching a heart
5.   ♣ A
6.   ♡ A
7.   ?

Declarer intended to play the ♡ A and ♡ K followed by the ♠ A and a spade. If spades were 2-2, then if the ♠ K hand had only two hearts, that hand would have to give a sluff and a ruff.

At trick six, East dropped the ♡ Q, giving declarer yet another option. It looked dangerous to cash the ♡ K, but if the ♡ Q were either singleton or from QJ doubleton, then the original line was still intact.

Declarer, therefore, played the ♠ A and another spade and when East won, he produced the "impossible" ♡ 7 for one down.

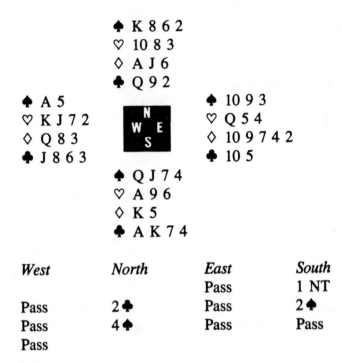

North - South vulnerable — East deals

```
                    ♠ K 8 6 2
                    ♡ 10 8 3
                    ◇ A J 6
                    ♣ Q 9 2
    ♠ A 5                          ♠ 10 9 3
    ♡ K J 7 2                      ♡ Q 5 4
    ◇ Q 8 3                        ◇ 10 9 7 4 2
    ♣ J 8 6 3                      ♣ 10 5
                    ♠ Q J 7 4
                    ♡ A 9 6
                    ◇ K 5
                    ♣ A K 7 4
```

West	North	East	South
		Pass	1 NT
Pass	2♣	Pass	2♠
Pass	4♠	Pass	Pass
Pass			

West started the ♡2 on the theory that with no good lead, he might as well hope to find a card in partner's hand that would at least be useful.

Declarer won the second heart and led the ♠Q won by the ace.

West judged East could have no high cards outside the ♡Q. But, East might have the ♠109.

West, therefore, cashed his heart trick and led the thirteenth heart.

```
              K 8 6
    5                     10 9
              J 7 4
```

This is the trump position when West led the last heart. East ruffed with the nine, forcing the jack. When declarer led to the dummy, he found himself having to guess whether to finesse for the ten or whether to drop it. This falsecard is rather rare and I admit I still have not found it, outside my imagination.

A similar fantasy.

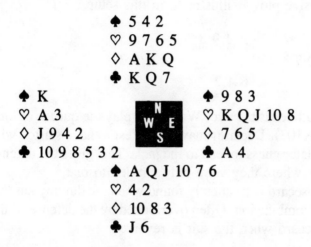

```
                ♠ 5 4 2
                ♡ 9 7 6 5
                ◇ A K Q
                ♣ K Q 7
   ♠ K                        ♠ 9 8 3
   ♡ A 3              N       ♡ K Q J 10 8
   ◇ J 9 4 2      W     E     ◇ 7 6 5
   ♣ 10 9 8 5 3 2     S       ♣ A 4
                ♠ A Q J 10 7 6
                ♡ 4 2
                ◇ 10 8 3
                ♣ J 6
```

How did the defense come to two trump tricks against 3 ♠? This one bears looking at. The play went:

1. ♡A
2. ♡K
3. Heart ruffed with the queen, allowed to win
4. Diamond to the Ace
5. Trump finesse, losing to the stiff king
6. Club to the ace
7. Now the fourth round of hearts left declarer wondering whether to ruff high or to ruff low

A J 9 8

6 4 2

Declarer's percentage play in this suit is to finesse the nine and if it loses to the king or queen, to repeat the finesse. A standard defensive ploy is illustrated in this setup.

```
              A J 9 8
                *
Q 10 7                     K 5 3
  *                          *
              6 4 2
                ★
```

When South leads the two, West must play the queen (or king if he has K107). Declarer may play West to have started with KQ7 and later guess to lead to the jack. This gives the defense two tricks where they were only entitled to one.

This falsecard is frequently found when the dummy has this high card combination. Often overlooked by the defense, is the same falsecard when the suit is reversed.

```
              6 4 2
                ★
K 5 3                      Q 10 7
                             *
              A J 9 8
```

If East plays the queen here, it is extremely likely that declarer will misguess.

Only when declarer has great length or where declarer is trying to guess the KJ combination does this falsecard work poorly. East has to determine each case of course, but on balance will come out way ahead by playing the queen.

Mildly similar to the above combination are these defensive possibilities.

```
              A K J 5 2
   Q 8 6 3                    7 4
              10 9
                ★
```

If South leads the nine or the ten, West must cover. Declarer, if he has no entry to dummy has to let the queen win unless he is absolutely desperate for tricks. West, therefore, should consider playing the queen from Qxxx, Qxx and Qx.

```
              A Q J 6 5 2
   K
              8 3
               ★
```

Declarer, as in the previous example, may feel obligated to duck this so as to keep an entry to dummy.

```
              A K J 7 6 5 2

              4 3
```

Declarer has a choice of safety plays here. He can finesse the jack, catering to all 3-1 or 2-2 splits, or he can duck the trick entirely which caters to all 3-1, 2-2, plus 4-0 if it's onside. If West has Q1098, he can play the queen to tempt declarer.

No one vulnerable — East deals

```
                    ♠ 4
                    ♡ 7 5
                    ◇ 8 5 3
                    ♣ A K J 7 6 5 2
    ♠ 9 6 3                         ♠ K J 10 8 7 5 2
    ♡ K J 9          N              ♡ Q 10 8
    ◇ K Q J       W     E           ◇ 10 9 7
    ♣ Q 10 9 8       S              ♣ —
                    ♠ A Q
                    ♡ A 6 4 3 2
                    ◇ A 6 4 2
                    ♣ 4 3
```

West	North	East	South
		3 ♠	3 NT
4 ♠	4 NT	Pass	Pass
Double	Pass	Pass	Pass

West leads the ♠9 to East's king and declarer's ace. Since 4 NT doubled should be worth making, declarer led a club, intending to duck whatever West played. West put in the queen, testing declarer's resolve.

This is the kind of situation that tries one nerves. Making 4 NT doubled is obviously a fine score, but making an overtrick does smooth ruffled egos. Should South duck the queen and take the profit or should he go for the gratification and bragging rights? What would you do?

The Idiot's Delight

There is a family of falsecards appropriately named to describe the feelings of a declarer who has fallen victim to one.

In general, the theme is always the same. Declarer's suit is dividing favorably and has no losers through normal play. The defense, however, by squandering its honors, may create a finessing position where one really shouldn't exist.

This is easier to show by example than by description.

```
                  K 10 8 6 2
                      *
     Q 5                      J 9
     *                         *
                  A 7 4 3
                      ★
```

West drops the queen on the ace. When declarer leads the three, it appears that he has a finesse versus drop choice.

Hardly. This shouldn't work, but since it is free, it can't hurt to try.

Something the defense can do which is guaranteed to irritate a declarer, is this.

```
                  K 10 8 6 2
                      *
     Q J 9                    3
     *                        *
                  A 7 5 4
                      ★
```

Declarer will suspect the dreaded "IDIOT'S DELIGHT" and will reject it by going up with the king.

The defense won't gain a trick by this, but you can imagine the satisfaction of watching declarer simmering away.

Be careful though, that the suit is not distributed thusly:

```
                  K 10 8 6 2
                      *
     Q J 9                    —      oops!
     *
                  A 7 5 4 3
                      ★
    _____

                  A K 10 8 6 2
                       *
     J 4                       Q 5
     *                          *
                  9 7 3
                      ★
```

The only finesse after the first trick should be in declarer's mind. But it has been known to work.

123

                    K 9 7 4
      J 2   Q 10
                    A 8 6 5 3

A slight change as the defense leads the suit first. This coup position may work because it is barely possible that West would lead the jack from J102.

                    K Q 8 2
      J 9 3   10 7 5
                    A 6 4

This one takes an extra trick to develop. Declarer leads the king and ace fetching the jack and nine from West. Now, it appears to declarer that he has to finesse.

Even more believable, from declarer's point of view, is for West to lead the jack to declarer's ace and then to play the nine when declarer leads to dummy.

Not quite in the family of "IDIOT'S DELIGHT," but still related is this one.

                    Q 9 8 2
      7 5 4   J 10 6
                    A K 3

When declarer leads the two, many defenders go up with the ten, hoping declarer has A43 instead of AK3. If East can tell that declarer has AK3, it is more effective for the defense to play the six in the East position.

If, however, East has Jx or 10x as in this combination, East has a very effective falsecard available.

$$\text{Q 9 8 2} \atop \clubsuit$$

10 7 5 4   J 6
♣   ♣

A K 3
♣

When declarer next plays the ace and leads to dummy, he is likely to credit East with J106 rather than J6, since most defenders would have J106 for the play of the jack.

East must be quite sure of the position to try this falsecard since it can be costly if declarer has Axx, Kxx, or Kxxx.

Q 9 8 2
♣

A 10 5 3   J 6
♣   ♣

K 7 4
♣

The defense has two tricks unless East plays his jack prematurely.

PART II

FALSECARDS BY DECLARER

However many falsecards were available to the defenders, and however complex they may have been, they were limited in their scope by the sad fact that each defender has a partner. As effective as a falsecard may have been, it always ran the danger that partner could be caught up in its deceit as well as declarer.

Declarer is bound by no such considerations. The only people looking at these cards and drawing conclusions from them are the enemy and they are fair game.

How sweet it is to know that your web will snare only gullible opponents and never a trusting partner!

Chapter 8

FALSECARDS AT TRICK ONE

It has often been said that hasty play at trick one is the most frequent declarer error. Certainly true. What has not been said is that failure to falsecard at trick one is the specific error most frequently made.

From the above, you might think that defensive falsecards are not as important as declarer's falsecards. Not true. On the average, a defensive falsecard is more likely to gain something than a falsecard by declarer. But this is fully compensated for by the fact that declarer can falsecard from five to ten times as often as a defender.

When does declarer have to start thinking about falsecards? At trick one, of course.

I would estimate that a conniving declarer will perform as much deception at trick one as on the rest of the hand. The number of things declarer can do are amazing.

At trick one, declarer's decisions will include, among others, whether to win the trick in dummy, whether to win the trick in hand, what card to win with, or perhaps, whether to win the trick at all.

Some of the time, declarer has no option, i.e., he better win or else.

```
              A 8 2
                  *
     7                      J
     *                      *
              Q 5 4
```

If declarer doesn't win his queen, he doesn't get it.

4 2
   *

5   Q
★   *

K 7

Again, no choice.

Frequently though, declarer will have a real option.

Here are a few of them. Note that the following discussion is of a general nature. Note also that your correct play will vary according to whether you are playing in notrump or a suit contract.

IN A NOTRUMP CONTRACT

5 2
  *

6   J
★   *

A K 7
?

If declarer chooses to win the trick, he should usually win with the king. Whenever declarer wins the first round of a suit with the ace, the defenders may question why declarer isn't holding up. The answer tends to be that declarer has a second stopper, i.e., the AK, or even AKQ.

If declarer wins with the king, the defense can't be as confident about declarer's holding. If declarer had Kx opposite xxx, he would have no choice but to win.

IN A SUIT CONTRACT

5 2
  *

6   J
★   *

A K 7

If declarer wins with the king, it will announce that he also has the ace. Why? Because if East had it, he would take the trick, and if West had it, he would not underlead it. If declarer wins with the king, each defender will know for the above reasons that declarer has the ace. If declarer wins trick one with the ace, the defenders may suspect strongly what is going on, but they won't know. They will only think they know. Somewhere in the back of their minds, there will be the seed of doubt.

```
              4 2
               *
  7                        J
  *                        *
              K Q 5
```

This combination occurs only at notrump. It's normal to win with the king trying to induce West to lead the suit again if he gets in. West may think East has the queen.

```
              4 2
               *
  7                        J
  *                        *
              K Q
```

Usually, you win the queen. The idea is to convince West you have the king. Hopefully he will try to get his partner in for a lead through your king. In practice, you can win with the king or the queen when holding KQ or KQx.

Both plays will give West something to think about.

```
              A 6 2
               *
  7                        10
  *                        *
              Q J 5
               *
```

Win with the queen. Leave West guessing who has the jack.

```
              A K 4 2
               *
  3                        9
  *                        *
              J 10 6
```

Win with the jack. West may talk himself into leading the suit again, giving you a fourth trick.

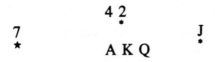

```
              4 2
                .

7                              J
.                              .
              A K Q
```

In a suit contract, it's generally best to win the ace on the stand-ard theory, that the defense knows you have it. At notrump, you should win with the king.

There is a useful principle here. When you have a three-card sequence, and can win the trick at trick one, you should win with the middle card.

```
              6 4 2
                .

7                              10
.                              .
              K Q J
                .
```

If you win with the queen, West may not know he can safely continue the suit.

```
              6 4 2
                .

A 9 8 7                        J 10 5
.                              .
              K Q 3
                .
```

This is the combination you want West to think exists. If West believes this to be the case, he may switch, giving you time.

```
              7 2
                .

5                              10
.                              .
              A Q J
                .
```

Declarer must falsecard with the queen. If LHO gains the lead, he will often continue this suit in the hope East has the jack.

```
               7 2
               *
K 9 6 5 3                    J 10 4
   *                            *
               A Q 8
                 *
```

This could easily be the situation from West's point of view.
Not an easy guess for West to make.

There are many falsecards available to declarer and there
are almost as many reasons for making a falsecard. Among the
most common are:

1.   The opponents have led your best suit
2.   When a ruff is threatened
3.   To fake a holdup
4.   To camouflage a stiff ace
5.   The anti-falsecard falsecard
6.   To fake weakness in the suit led
7.   To disrupt the defenders' signals

The Opponents Have Led Your Best Suit

```
               8 2
               *
 5                           Q
 *                            *
               A K J 7 3
                   *
```

The opponents have surprised you by leading this suit. If you
intend to establish this suit yourself, you can duck the queen.
East may continue the suit to your advantage.

The reason you play the seven rather than the three, is that
you want East to think West has a five-card suit.

```
               8 2
               *
10 9 6 5                     Q 4
   *                           *
               A K J 7 3
                   *
```

If South plays the three, East will know declarer has five since
the five will be readable as from a four-card suit. If declarer

131

plays the seven, East can easily come to the conclusion that West has the three, and consequently a five bagger.

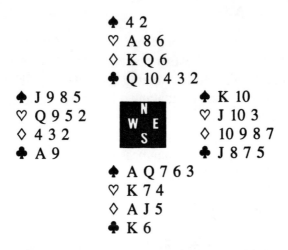

♠ 4 2
♡ A 8 6
◊ K Q 6
♣ Q 10 4 3 2

♠ J 9 8 5
♡ Q 9 5 2
◊ 4 3 2
♣ A 9

♠ K 10
♡ J 10 3
◊ 10 9 8 7
♣ J 8 7 5

♠ A Q 7 6 3
♡ K 7 4
◊ A J 5
♣ K 6

South opened 1 NT, hiding his spade suit and North raised to 3 NT.

This action by South could have been wrong. But not this time, as West chose the ♠5, East playing the king.

Declarer has no sure route to nine tricks although there are lots of possibilities. The problem with ducking the spade is that the defense may switch to hearts. Nonetheless, declarer did duck the spade, falsecarding with the six, as in the previous example. When East continued spades, declarer had time to establish a long spade plus a club trick.

Note again the importance of South's falsecard in spades. If South had played the three, East would have recognized that South had five spades. East might have decided to shift and he might have found a heart shift.

There is a second family of hands where the opponents attack one of your strong holdings. It may be possible for you to make them think they have found your weak spot when, in fact, your real worry is elsewhere.

Combinations like this are common.

No one vulnerable — South deals

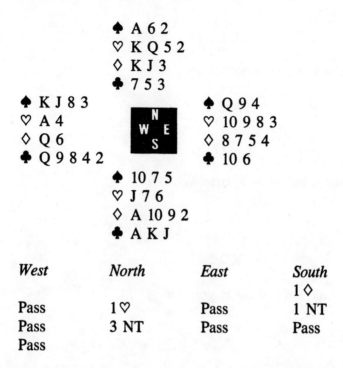

```
                    ♠ A 6 2
                    ♡ K Q 5 2
                    ◇ K J 3
                    ♣ 7 5 3
   ♠ K J 8 3                      ♠ Q 9 4
   ♡ A 4          N               ♡ 10 9 8 3
   ◇ Q 6       W     E            ◇ 8 7 5 4
   ♣ Q 9 8 4 2    S               ♣ 10 6
                    ♠ 10 7 5
                    ♡ J 7 6
                    ◇ A 10 9 2
                    ♣ A K J
```

West	North	East	South
			1 ◇
Pass	1 ♡	Pass	1 NT
Pass	3 NT	Pass	Pass
Pass			

West leads the ♣4. Declarer has nine tricks if he can guess the diamonds or if the hearts are 3-3. There is no guarantee of nine tricks though, except via a good guess.

South decided on a simple subterfuge. Winning the first trick with the king, he followed with a diamond to the king and a finesse into West's queen. West, expecting his partner to have the ♣J, continued clubs giving declarer a second chance at three club tricks.

This gave declarer nine tricks plus the time to get at them.

Had declarer won the ♣J at trick one, West might have shifted to a spade and that would have been an effective defense.

There are many, many such combinations where declarer can hide his true strength in the suit led.

```
          8 2
6                    J
        A K Q
```

This one we've seen before.

```
          A 5 2
6                    J
        K Q 4
```

Routine, but often overlooked.

```
          A 5 2
6                   10
        K J 5
```

Use this when West is going to get in.

```
          J 10 3
7                    5
        A K 4
```

Likewise.

```
          J 10 4
7                    5
        A Q 2
```

Likewise.

```
          Q 10 4
7                    5
        A J 3
```

And likewise. In all these cases, the defenders may be able to see through your falsecard if their signaling methods are worked out. But even in high level bridge, defenders are prone to careless play when they think they know what's going on.

Both vulnerable — South deals

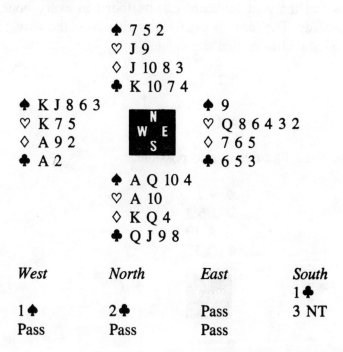

```
                    ♠ 7 5 2
                    ♡ J 9
                    ◇ J 10 8 3
                    ♣ K 10 7 4
    ♠ K J 8 6 3                   ♠ 9
    ♡ K 7 5          N            ♡ Q 8 6 4 3 2
    ◇ A 9 2      W       E        ◇ 7 6 5
    ♣ A 2            S            ♣ 6 5 3
                    ♠ A Q 10 4
                    ♡ A 10
                    ◇ K Q 4
                    ♣ Q J 9 8
```

West	North	East	South
			1♣
1♠	2♣	Pass	3 NT
Pass	Pass	Pass	

West had no reason not to lead a spade and did start with the six, to East's nine and declarer's queen. West took the first club trick, thinking his partner had the ♠10, and tried to set up the spade suit by leading the king.

Declarer had no problems now and ended up with nine tricks. Had declarer won the ♠10, West would have no choice but to hope for a miracle. A heart shift, though made in desperation, would have resulted in down three.

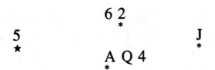

This and the next falsecard can be found in every book on falsecards. The idea, as usual, is to give West the wrong impression and hope that the defense errs.

```
            6 2
  5                     J
            A Q
```

Something like this is also possible.

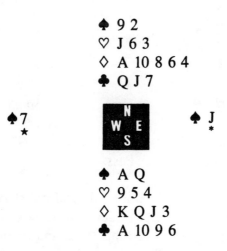

♠ 9 2
♡ J 6 3
◇ A 10 8 6 4
♣ Q J 7

♠ 7

♠ J

♠ A Q
♡ 9 5 4
◇ K Q J 3
♣ A 10 9 6

3 NT by South.

If you win the queen and later take a losing club finesse, the defense may switch to hearts.

For the strong of heart, you can win the ♠A, lead the ◇J to the ace and take the club finesse.

If West wins, he is supposed to lead a small spade to his partner's queen.

Looks good in spirit. Might even be good at the table.

Memory doesn't serve me to well (disasters are easily forgotten), but when I tried this ploy, the East-West hands were something like this.

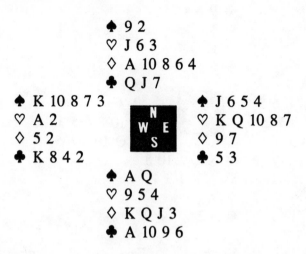

♠ 9 2
♡ J 6 3
◇ A 10 8 6 4
♣ Q J 7

♠ K 10 8 7 3
♡ A 2
◇ 5 2
♣ K 8 4 2

♠ J 6 5 4
♡ K Q 10 8 7
◇ 9 7
♣ 5 3

♠ A Q
♡ 9 5 4
◇ K Q J 3
♣ A 10 9 6

West took his ♣K, the ♠K, three more spades, and five more hearts. Down six!

Some falsecards similar to the above, but not as blatant, may seem to give up a trick, but seldom do.

A 4 2
*

5
*

10
*

K J 7
*

If West next gets in, he is very likely to lead this suit again, thinking East has the jack.

Both vulnerable — North deals.

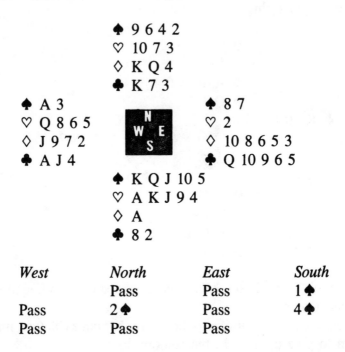

<pre>
                    ♠ 9 6 4 2
                    ♡ 10 7 3
                    ◊ K Q 4
                    ♣ K 7 3
  ♠ A 3   ♠ 8 7
  ♡ Q 8 6 5   N   ♡ 2
  ◊ J 9 7 2   W   E   ◊ 10 8 6 5 3
  ♣ A J 4   S   ♣ Q 10 9 6 5
                    ♠ K Q J 10 5
                    ♡ A K J 9 4
                    ◊ A
                    ♣ 8 2
</pre>

West	North	East	South
	Pass	Pass	1♠
Pass	2♠	Pass	4♠
Pass	Pass	Pass	

West leads the ♡5. Declarer, fearing a ruff but not knowing for sure which opponent has the singleton, can try this.

Play dummy's ten and when not covered, overtake with the jack. Now lead the ♠J or ♠Q.

West will have to see through two falsecards. He will have to take his ♠A (risking that East has a stiff king) and then he will have to lead another heart.

```
              A 6 2
                  *
  5                       8
  *                       *
              Q 10 9
                  *
```

This falsecard does lose a trick, but if declarer can't stand for the defense to switch suits, it can be a good investment.

Even stranger is this one.

No one vulnerable — North deals

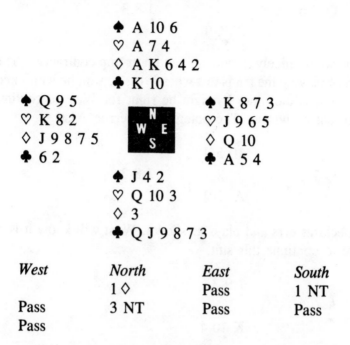

♠ A 10 6
♡ A 7 4
◇ A K 6 4 2
♣ K 10

♠ Q 9 5   ♠ K 8 7 3
♡ K 8 2   ♡ J 9 6 5
◇ J 9 8 7 5   ◇ Q 10
♣ 6 2   ♣ A 5 4

♠ J 4 2
♡ Q 10 3
◇ 3
♣ Q J 9 8 7 3

West	North	East	South
	1 ◇	Pass	1 NT
Pass	3 NT	Pass	Pass
Pass			

West didn't want to lead a diamond since North had bid them. Instead, he guessed to lead the ♡2.

Declarer ducked in dummy, hoping East would win with the king. This would have left the ♡Q as a later entry to the clubs.

When East played the jack, declarer no longer had his entry so he tried some thievery instead.

South let the jack win. When East continued with the ♡5, South played the ten and West covered, thinking East had the ♡Q.

This led to ten tricks for South, where he might have been held to six.

Finally, some odd combinations with lots of potential to confuse.

```
                10 5 4
                  ♣
Q 7 6 2                        J 8 3
    ♠                            ♣
                A K 9
                  ♣
```

This works nicely in both suit and notrump contracts. The effect of playing the ten is that when West gets in, he won't know if East has the nine. It might be right for West to continue. It might be wrong. The potential for error exists.

```
                10 5 4
                  ♣
Q 7 6 2                        J 8 3
    ♠                            ♣
                A K 9
                  ♣
```

If declarer errs and plays as shown, West will know it is not safe to continue this suit.

```
                J 9 3
                  ♣
5                              2
♠                              ♣
                K 10 4
                   ♣
```

Against opponents who don't have clear definition in their signals, West may try to drop your king rather than put East in for a lead through.

```
                Q 9 8
                  ♣
4                              10
♠                              ♣
                K J 3
                  ♣
```

This falsecard is intended to induce West to underlead his ace when he gets in.

North - South vulnerable — South deals

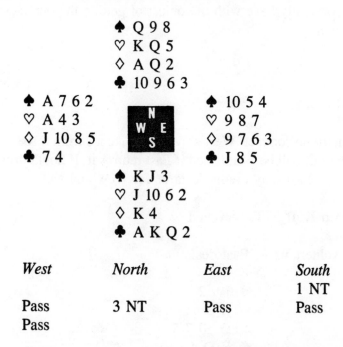

	♠ Q 9 8	
	♡ K Q 5	
	◊ A Q 2	
	♣ 10 9 6 3	

West	North	East	South
			1 NT
Pass	3 NT	Pass	Pass
Pass			

West leads the ♠2 to the ten and king. Declarer has twelve likely tricks, but he also has two losers. However, if he can steal a spade trick (after knocking out the ♡A), he may still get twelve tricks.

As it is, when West wins the ♡A, he is likely, with some justification, to underlead the ♠A again, hoping for this.

```
            Q 9 8
A 7 6 2                    J 10 4
            K 5 3
```

If this did exist, declarer might duck, thus losing three spades.

If declarer had won trick one with the jack, there would have been no chance at twelve tricks.

141

A curious falsecard exists where you imply greater strength than you really have with the object of getting the opponents to switch.

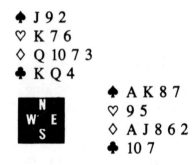

```
          J 9 7
           *
  5                      A
  *                      *
          K 6 2
           *
```

At a notrump contract, West's five looks like it's from Q1085(x) and the suit will be established if East returns it. If South drops the king, East may credit declarer for KQx and shift.

When a Ruff is Threatened

Both vulnerable — East deals

```
          ♠ J 9 2
          ♡ K 7 6
          ◊ Q 10 7 3
          ♣ K Q 4
                        ♠ A K 8 7
          N             ♡ 9 5
        W   E           ◊ A J 8 6 2
          S             ♣ 10 7
```

West	North	East	South
		1 ◊	1 ♡
Pass	2 ♡	Pass	4 ♡
Pass	Pass	Pass	

West leads the ◊ 5. How should East defend?

The answer to this depends on what declarer plays. If South plays the four, then the five can be a singleton and a diamond return would be reasonable.

If declarer plays the nine, then the five could have been from 54 doubleton or it could still be a singleton. East's guess!

142

This problem is one which I guarantee will come up at least once per session.

Whether East solves it depends on good guesswork UNLESS declarer gives the defense a free ride.

Here's the complete hand.

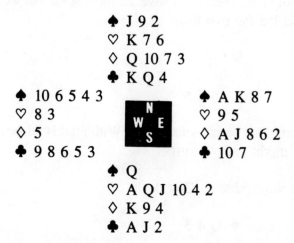

This situation comes up repeatedly. From declarer's point of view, a potential singleton is led.

The rule for declarer is always: IF POSSIBLE, CONCEAL A SPOT CARD SMALLER THAN THE ONE LED.

On this hand, the rule directs declarer to play the nine. East will wonder where the four is, but since he can't tell for sure, he will often do the wrong thing. On this hand, if East switches to the ♠K, the contract will become unbeatable.

Here are many such falsecards. In each of the examples, the card led is known or suspected to be a singleton and declarer wants to persuade East otherwise.

```
            Q 10 6 3
                  *
   4                      A J 9 8 7 5
   *                            *
            K 2
            *
```

If the four and two were exchanged, this play should not work.

```
          Q 10 6 3
                *
2                        A J 9 8 7 5
*                               *
          K 4
           *
```

You can try this but East won't be fooled very often. From East's point of view, West can't have the four, since that would mean he had led the two from 42.

```
          Q 4 3
               *
2                        A J 9 7 5
*                               *
          K 10 8 6
               *
```

This is extreme, but perhaps necessary. Without this falsecard, the defense might get two ruffs.

East - West vulnerable — East deals.

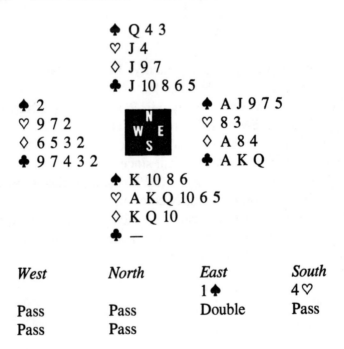

```
                ♠ Q 4 3
                ♡ J 4
                ◇ J 9 7
                ♣ J 10 8 6 5
♠ 2                           ♠ A J 9 7 5
♡ 9 7 2         N             ♡ 8 3
◇ 6 5 3 2     W   E           ◇ A 8 4
♣ 9 7 4 3 2     S             ♣ A K Q
                ♠ K 10 8 6
                ♡ A K Q 10 6 5
                ◇ K Q 10
                ♣ —
```

West	North	East	South
		1♠	4♡
Pass	Pass	Double	Pass
Pass	Pass		

In this setting, South must falsecard else the defense get three spades plus one diamond.

$$
\begin{array}{ccc}
 & \text{J 8 4 ♣} & \\
\text{2 ♠} & & \text{A Q 9 7 6 5 ♣} \\
 & \text{K 10 3 ♣} &
\end{array}
$$

Notice this would not work if the three and two were exchanged.

$$
\begin{array}{ccc}
 & \text{J 10 6 3 ♣} & \\
\text{A Q 9 8 4 2 ♠} & & \text{7 ♣} \\
 & \text{K 5 ♣} &
\end{array}
$$

Similar to the above.

$$
\begin{array}{ccc}
 & \text{K 8 5 4 ♣} & \\
\text{6 ♠} & & \text{A Q 7 3 2 ♣} \\
 & \text{J 10 9 ♠} &
\end{array}
$$

The ten is a mandatory falsecard. Declarer is trying to imply that West has J96 which would be consistent with the opening lead. If South plays the nine or the jack, it would mean West had led the six from J106 or 1096 since the correct lead from J106 is the jack, and from 1096, the ten, East would work out that the six was a singleton.

$$
\begin{array}{ccc}
 & \text{K 7 6 2 ♣} & \\
\text{5 ♠} & & \text{A 9 8 4 3 ♣} \\
 & \text{Q J 10 ♣} &
\end{array}
$$

Exactly the same considerations apply as in the previous example. South must play specifically the jack. East can believe that West would lead the five from Q105. If South played, say, the queen, East would not believe the falsecard since that would mean West had led from J105. With this holding he would have started with the jack.

To Fake a Holdup

When the defense gets off to its most effective defense, declarer is sometimes able to borrow time by using a rather unusual holdup.

For example:

```
                J 10 7
                  *
    8 5                       K Q 9 4 3
     *                            *
                A 6 2
                  *
```

If declarer wins the first trick with the ace, the defenders will run the suit when West gets in to lead it.

But, if declarer ducks the opening lead, the defenders will experience difficulty getting the suit going. East won't be able to lead the suit himself. He will have to wait until West can lead the suit again and even then, East will require an additional entry. Time. A tempo. this is what declarer gains by this holdup.

There are many such situations where declarer can gain time.

```
                Q 10 3
                  *
    8 4                       K J 9 7 2
     *                            *
                A 6 5
                  *
```

In each of these four diagrams, declarer can gain a tempo by playing as indicated.

East, in each case, will be unable to continue the suit without losing a trick.

```
                J 9 4
                  *
    10 7                       K Q 8 6 2
     *                            *
                A 5 3
                  *
    ─────────────────────────────────────
                Q 6 2
                  *
    7 4                        K J 10 9 5
     *                            *
                A 8 3
                  *
```

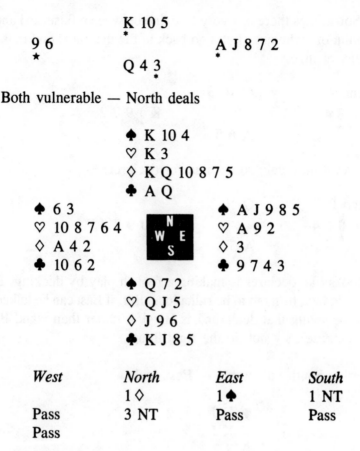

K 10 5

9 6 ♣ A J 8 7 2
♠ Q 4 3 ♣
♣

Both vulnerable — North deals

♠ K 10 4
♡ K 3
◇ K Q 10 8 7 5
♣ A Q

♠ 6 3   ♠ A J 9 8 5
♡ 10 8 7 6 4   ♡ A 9 2
◇ A 4 2   ◇ 3
♣ 10 6 2   ♣ 9 7 4 3

♠ Q 7 2
♡ Q J 5
◇ J 9 6
♣ K J 8 5

West	North	East	South
	1 ◇	1 ♠	1 NT
Pass	3 NT	Pass	Pass
Pass			

West leads the ♠6.

If declarer plays the four or ten, East will just cover. Say, for example, that declarer plays the four. East will play the eight, losing to declarer's queen. When West takes the ◇ A, another spade will lead to down two.

By comparison, if South plays the king, East will win, but he will not be able to continue spades.

West will take his ◇ A but the spades won't yet be good. Ten tricks for declarer. A swing of three tricks for declarer's tempo-creating play.

So far, none of these examples have been falsecards. They have been examples of technique.

Sometimes there is a very fine line between a falsecard and a point of technique. Let's go back to the diagrams and make a tiny change.

Hand A   Q 10 3

  8 4   K J 9 7 2

              A 6 5

Ducking may gain some time for declarer.

Hand B   Q 10 3

  8 6 4   K J 9 7 2

              A 5

It looks like declarer is making a foolish play by ducking. It may, in fact, turn out to be ridiculous. But, if East can be talked into believing that declarer has Hand A rather than Hand B, the defense may not do the right thing.

North - South vulnerable — East deals.

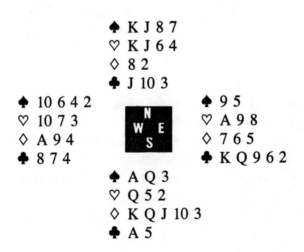

West	North	East	South
		Pass	1 NT
Pass	2♣	Double	2◇
Pass	3 NT	Pass	Pass
Pass			

West leads the ♣8.

At trick one, dummy plays the ten and East the queen. If declarer takes this, he will go down for sure. West will get in eventually and a second club lead would do it.

If South ducks the first club, East can set 3 NT by leading a small club. But will he? How can he tell? Quite likely, he won't be able to work out the situation and will switch to a diamond.

Nine tricks for South.

There are quite a few of these phony holdups. Here is a partial list.

```
              Q 10 3
                 ♣
   8                        J
   ★                        ♣
              A 6
                 ♣
         ─────────────────────
              Q 7 2
                 ♣
   5                        8
   ★                        ♣
              A 4
                 ♣
```

You would need to know from the auction that East had this suit.

```
              K 10 4
                 ♣
   9                        A
   ★                        ♣
              Q 3
                 ♣
```

Will East know he can continue with a small card?

To Camouflage a Stiff Ace

When you have a singleton ace in the suit led by the defense, you will often have the opportunity to mess with the opponents' signaling.

Look at the following setup from West's point of view.

$$\begin{matrix} & 10\ 4\ 3 & \\ & * & \\ K\ 7\ 6\ 5\ 2 & & 8 \\ * & & * \\ & A & \\ & * & \end{matrix}$$

West can see that East has QJ98 and declarer, therefore, a singleton ace.

When West gets in, it may be important to know that the defense has or does not have a trick coming in this suit.

Compare with this setup.

$$\begin{matrix} & 10\ 4\ 3 & \\ & * & \\ K\ 7\ 6\ 5\ 2 & & J \\ * & & * \\ & A & \\ & * & \end{matrix}$$

What can West tell about this suit?

It looks like East has the queen, but the eight and nine can be anywhere. East's holding can be any of the following:

> QJ
> QJ9
> QJ8
> QJ98

Four possible holdings: four chances therefore, for the defense to misjudge and do the wrong thing.

Remember, if you offer enough bait, you will eventually catch something.

What this means is that when you are declaring a hand and

the opponents lead your singleton ace suit, you should not routinely play dummy's small card.

These are all possible plays which may cause the defense to err.

```
            10 4 2
   7          *
   *          A
```

This play, as just seen, may prevent the defense from getting an early count in this suit.

```
            J 6 2
   7          *
   *          A
```

Likewise.

```
            Q 6 2
   7          *
   *          A
```

If you have no possible use for the queen, this play may (if East covers) convince the defense you have a loser in this suit.

Both vulnerable — South deals

```
                      ♠ Q 6 2
                      ♡ 10 8 5 4
                      ◊ K J 8 2
                      ♣ 6 4
        ♠ J 9 8 7 3                      ♠ K 10 5 4
        ♡ J 7 2            N             ♡ Q 3
        ◊ Q 9 5 3      W       E         ◊ A 7 6 4
        ♣ 7                S             ♣ 9 5 2
                      ♠ A
                      ♡ A K 9 6
                      ◊ 10
                      ♣ A K Q J 10 8 3
```

West	North	East	South
			2♣
Pass	2◊	Pass	3♣
Pass	3◊	Pass	3♡
Pass	4♡	Pass	6♡
Pass	Pass	Pass	

The bidding could have been better. I've certainly seen worse, however.

West leads the ♠7. If declarer plays without thought and follows with dummy's two, East will use the Rule of Eleven and will play the five.

When West gets in with his heart trick, there's little chance he will try to cash a spade trick. After all, wouldn't South play the queen if he had a second spade?

If declarer plays dummy's queen at trick one, East will have no option but to cover and West will have no obvious reason to do the right thing.

```
              Q J 2
  7            *
  *            A
```

If declarer can afford it, he can try playing the jack or queen. East might cover. If you have entries, however, it might be better to play the two. This will allow you to set up a trick later.

```
              J 10 4
  7            *
  *            A
```

If East covers, you have achieved a stopper where none should exist. In the following hand, that might be crucial.

No one vulnerable — North deals

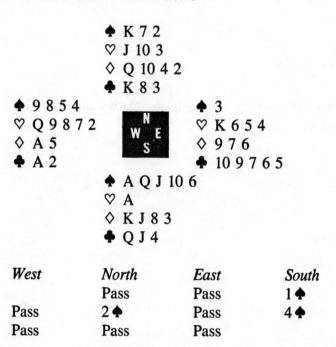

```
                 ♠ K 7 2
                 ♡ J 10 3
                 ◇ Q 10 4 2
                 ♣ K 8 3
  ♠ 9 8 5 4                    ♠ 3
  ♡ Q 9 8 7 2                  ♡ K 6 5 4
  ◇ A 5                        ◇ 9 7 6
  ♣ A 2                        ♣ 10 9 7 6 5
                 ♠ A Q J 10 6
                 ♡ A
                 ◇ K J 8 3
                 ♣ Q J 4
```

West	North	East	South
	Pass	Pass	1 ♠
Pass	2 ♠	Pass	4 ♠
Pass	Pass	Pass	

West leads the ♡7. It looks like declarer should make 5♠ routinely by drawing trump and conceding two aces.

With trumps being 4-1, things aren't quite so easy.

If declarer plays dummy's three, East can use the Rule of Eleven and conclude to play low to declarer's ace. Now when West wins his aces, he can lead hearts, forcing declarer to ruff, thus establishing another trick for the defense.

If declarer plays dummy's jack, East may cover. This will create a second heart stopper which means the defense won't be able to tap declarer.

Note that I have commented on two previous hands that the Rule of Eleven was helping the defenders. If the defenders were using different lead methods, the suggested falsecard will still contribute to the defensive difficulties.

The principles above can be extended to include situations like these.

```
                 10 4 2
     6                          J
                 A K
```

The play may give the defense hope, psychologically, or logically, that you have losers in this suit.

```
                 J 4 2
     6                          Q
                 A K
```

Likewise.

East - West vulnerable — South deals

```
                    ♠ J 6 2
                    ♡ K Q 4 3
                    ◇ K 10 7 3
                    ♣ Q 4
   ♠ 9 3                            ♠ Q 10 8 7 5 4
   ♡ 5              N               ♡ A 9
   ◇ 9 8 5 4      W   E             ◇ A 6
   ♣ K 9 7 6 5 2    S               ♣ J 8 3
                    ♠ A K
                    ♡ J 10 8 7 6 2
                    ◇ Q J 2
                    ♣ A 10
```

West	North	East	South
			1♡
Pass	3♡	Pass	4♡
Pass	Pass	Pass	

West started with the ♣9. If declarer puts up the jack, East will cover and declarer will win.

When East takes his ♡A, he will have a tough decision. A spade continuation could be right, but so could a club shift.

I'm inclined to think that if South plays the ♣J, East will return a spade most of the time.

On this hand, it would be wrong.

The Anti-Falsecard Falsecard

In the section on defenders' falsecards, this specific situation was noted

155

$$9\ 5\ 4$$
$$J\ 8\ 6\ 3 \qquad\qquad A\ K\ 7$$
$$Q\ 10\ 2$$

Against a suit contract, the defense can give declarer a headache if East wins his ace and returns the seven. Declarer will misguess more often than not.

Declarer can sometimes produce a falsecard of his own which makes it hard or impossible for the defense to try this ploy.

$$9\ 5\ 4$$
$$J\ 8\ 6\ 3 \qquad\qquad A\ K\ 7$$
$$Q\ 10\ 2$$

If declarer can afford it, he can drop the ten spot. This will look to East as if South has Q10 doubleton and West J8632.

If this is the case, then East should not underlead his king.

If declarer does drop the ten and if East does return a small card, then declarer can surely play low and not worry that the defense is executing a swindle.

Variations on this combination include:

$$9\ 4\ 2$$
$$5 \qquad\qquad A$$
$$Q\ 10\ 3$$

$$10\ 4\ 2$$
$$5 \qquad\qquad A$$
$$Q\ 9\ 3$$

$$6\ 4\ 2$$
$$5 \qquad\qquad A$$
$$Q\ 10\ 3$$

In this setting, you can't afford to play the ten. That would lose a trick any time East had the jack.

Falsecards by Declarer to Fake Weakness in the Suit Led

You can try this one at either suit or notrump contracts.

```
            A 3
  4          *
  *         K J 7
```

By rising with the ace, you will appear to deny holding the KJ. Logically, if you had the KJx you would let the lead come around to your hand.

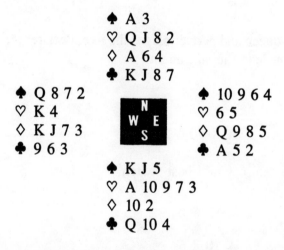

```
                ♠ A 3
                ♡ Q J 8 2
                ◇ A 6 4
                ♣ K J 8 7
  ♠ Q 8 7 2            ♠ 10 9 6 4
  ♡ K 4          N     ♡ 6 5
  ◇ K J 7 3    W   E   ◇ Q 9 8 5
  ♣ 9 6 3         S    ♣ A 5 2
                ♠ K J 5
                ♡ A 10 9 7 3
                ◇ 10 2
                ♣ Q 10 4
```

Against 4 ♡, West led the ♠2. This free finesse does South no good. Rather than make the automatic play of bringing the lead to his hand, declarer went up with the ♠A and finessed in hearts.

Was West clearly wrong to continue spades? He did and declarer had time to set up the clubs for a diamond discard.

To Disrupt the Defenders' Signals

Without exception, the most potent falsecards in bridge occur at trick one when declarer plays from his hand.

Some of these falsecards were discussed earlier, i.e., winning with an unusual card so as to misrepresent your strength.

The most effective falsecards, however, are not the big, brazen ones. They are the subtle ones where you play a two instead of a four. Or a six, instead of a three.

Take this situation from West's point of view.

AT NOTRUMP

```
                    4 3
                     *
    Q J 9 7                        5
      *                            *
                    6
                    *
```

You lead the queen and partner played the five, declarer the six. Should you lead the suit again?

```
                    4 3
    Q J 9 7                        8 5
                A K 10 6 2
```

If this is the setup, you'd best switch.

```
                    4 3
    Q J 9 7                        K 5 2
                A 10 8 6
```

BUT, if this is the actual holding, it is correct to continue.

What West should do is not clear. What is clear is that declarer has created an illusion which is going to mislead the defenders rather frequently. What's scary is that it was so easy to do.

Declarer played a six instead of a two. Nothing fancy, nothing gaudy, but still effective.

Good defenders rely heavily on their communcations and that usually means good signaling methods with their spot cards.

As we've just seen, these signaling methods are not perfect.

The set of examples in this section are among the most important in the book. Their importance stems from many factors.

1. They work
2. They are easy to execute
3. They are common
4. The things that make them work can be used in many other situations.

```
              8 6 2
               *
K                           5
 *                           *
              Q 7 3
               *
```

This is the most common combination. The idea is that by playing the seven, you make it appear to West that his partner likes this suit.

```
              8 6 2
A K J 4                     10 9 5
              Q 7 3
```

This is the combination that actually exists. East is trying to discourage West.

```
              8 6 2
               *
A K J 4                     Q 5 3
    *                          *
             10 9 7
               *
```

This is the combination declarer wants West to think exists.

```
              Q 9 8
               *
A K 10 7 2                  5 3
     *                       *
              J 6 4
                ?
```

What should declarer play to keep the defenders from getting their third round to ruff?

If South plays the jack, West will note that both the three and the four are missing. If East has either one, the defense has a ruff coming. If East has neither, then the five will be a singleton (or J5 doubleton) and again, the defense will have a ruff coming.

The jack is 100% the wrong play.

If South plays the six, West will again note the three and four are missing, and will sort it out as above. The six is a worse play than the jack. The jack, at least, has shock value against careless opponents.

This leaves the four, which is correct. West can work it out, but it is not as obvious. It's possible East has J65 and West will cater to this on occasion.

Conversely.

```
              Q 9 8
                    *
   A K J 7 2                    10 6 4
        *                            *
              5 3
               ?
```

What should South play if he wants West to take his ace rather than to switch?

South should play the five. West may conclude East has 43 and wants a ruff.

There is an interesting rule you can apply in these situations.

When defense starts with a high card which wins, declarer can influence the opening leader's second play by doing this:

A. If declarer likes the lead, he should play a higher than necessary spot card. It may look to West as if his partner has the missing spot card and is encouraging.

B. If declarer hates the lead, he should play his lowest spot card. West *may* be talked out of continuing if he can't read his partner's card.

NOTE that it is easier to get your opponents to continue a suit than it is to get them to stop.

Here are some more variations on the above combination.

```
                    Q 9 8
                      *
    A K 10 7 2                    6 5 4
        *                           *
                    J 3
                     *
```

If South wants West to continue, he must drop the jack. This goes against the grain because the jack is the card that most players choose when they want West to *stop* leading the suit.

Nonetheless, the jack is the proper card. West will note the three is missing and may continue, hoping to give East a ruff.

Odd, isn't it, that declarers have been playing the wrong card for all these years.

```
                    Q 9 8
                      *
    A K 10 7 2                    4 3
        *                          *
                    J 6 5
                     ?
```

Doesn't matter. For declarer's play to make a difference, he has to have spot cards higher and lower than the one played by East.

Then, according to which spot card declarer plays, he will have "concealed" an important card.

In the above example, West will note that the three is missing. Whatever card South chooses, West will have the same amount of information to go on.

```
                    Q 9 8
                      *
    A K 10 7 2                    5 4
        *                          *
                    J 6 3
```

This is a repetition of an earlier example. If South plays the three, West will note the four is missing. If South plays the six, West will note that the four *and* three are missing. In other words, South's choice of cards can influence the number of pertinent cards that West is missing. Again, note that South has a spot higher than East's card, plus a spot lower than East's card.

```
              Q J 9
                 *
    A K 10 7 2              8 6
        *                    *
              5 4 3
               ?
```

Doesn't matter. Whichever card South chooses, West will see there are three smaller cards missing. South can do nothing to confuse the defense.

```
              Q 7 5
                 *
    A K J 10 6              3
        *                   *
              9 8 4 2
```

If South wants West to switch, South must play the two. Any other card will conceal the two. West, noting the two is missing, may conclude his partner has it. West will cash the ace and the defense will gets its ruff. Guaranteed.

If South plays the two, there is a fair chance West will switch.

```
              6 3
               *
    Q J 10 4              9 5
        *                 *
              A K 8 7 2
```

At notrump, South is hardly bothered by this lead. If South requires tricks in this suit, he should play the seven. West may continue, thinking East's five was encouraging.

Note that in this diagram, you are not gaining a trick. You are gaining time.

```
              K 3
 J 10 8 7      *                5
   *         A Q 9 6 4 2         *
```

Conceivably, you might duck this trick. For instance:

Both vulnerable — West deals

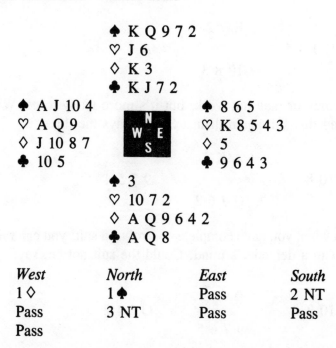

```
              ♠ K Q 9 7 2
              ♡ J 6
              ◇ K 3
              ♣ K J 7 2
♠ A J 10 4                      ♠ 8 6 5
♡ A Q 9          N             ♡ K 8 5 4 3
◇ J 10 8 7     W   E           ◇ 5
♣ 10 5           S             ♣ 9 6 4 3
              ♠ 3
              ♡ 10 7 2
              ◇ A Q 9 6 4 2
              ♣ A Q 8
```

West	North	East	South
West	*North*	*East*	*South*
1 ◇	1 ♠	Pass	2 NT
Pass	3 NT	Pass	Pass
Pass			

With the ◇ J lead, declarer can pretty well count on diamonds being 4-1. If declarer plays on diamonds, West will see declarer's diamond length and he will have gotten some signals from East. It's unlikely declarer will be allowed to get his nine tricks in time.

A better strategy is for declarer to duck the diamond lead in both hands, i.e.,

                    K 3

J 10 8 7   5

                    A Q 9 6 4 2

West is very likely to lead another diamond. Remember, even though he knows you have some high diamonds for your 2 NT bid, he doesn't know you have six of them.

                    K 7 2

Q J 9 5   A 6 4

                    10 8 3

This may or may not work, but it's more likely to get West to lead this suit again than if South plays the three.

                    A K 3

10 8   9 7 5 4

                    Q J 6 2

Even when you have complete control of a suit, you can raise doubt in a defender's mind. Could the suit not be, say:

                    A K 3

10 8   Q J 4 2

                    9 7 6 5

East can afford no better than the four.

This kind of falsecard is almost endless.

                    K Q 7

8   4

                    A 6 2

A little dust in their eyes.

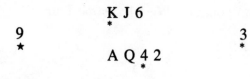

```
            K J 6
9                       3

            A Q 4 2
```

More dust.

```
            A K
10                      2

            Q J 7
```

Different and a little flagrant.

```
            Q J 3
A                       5

            K 10 4 2
```

More dust.

```
            A 7 3
K                       5

            Q 8 6 4 2
```

If West starts the king against a notrump contract, let him think he's on to a good thing.

So far, the falsecards in this section have been efforts to interfere with their attitude signals. You have tried to convince a defender that his partner likes the lead when actually, he doesn't. And vice versa.

Another useful, but less frequent falsecard by declarer, is one which tries to interrupt the defenders' count signals.

Against a notrump contract, West leads the four.

```
                J 9 2
                  ♣
    K 8 6 4                      A 5
        ♣                         ♣
                Q 10 7 3
                   ?
```

If declarer plays the three, East will realize West has led from a four-card suit. He may judge to switch.

Obviously, the suit West led is not a threat to South. If South wishes the defense to continue it, he should play the seven.

East will think, or hope, that West started with either Qxxxx or Kxxxx and is likely to return the five. This will do declarer's work and it may also gain declarer a tempo.

Chapter 9

FALSECARDS IN AND AROUND
THE TRUMP SUIT

Because of the special nature of trumps, there are some falsecards which are effective only when the trump suit is involved.

North - South vulnerable — South deals

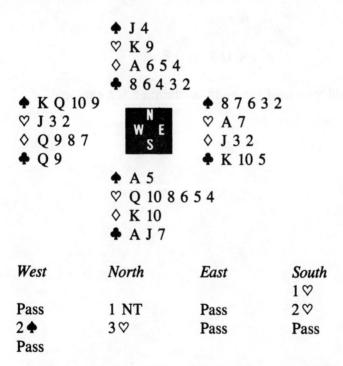

	♠ J 4	
	♡ K 9	
	◇ A 6 5 4	
	♣ 8 6 4 3 2	

♠ K Q 10 9		♠ 8 7 6 3 2
♡ J 3 2	N W E S	♡ A 7
◇ Q 9 8 7		◇ J 3 2
♣ Q 9		♣ K 10 5

	♠ A 5	
	♡ Q 10 8 6 5 4	
	◇ K 10	
	♣ A J 7	

West	North	East	South
			1 ♡
Pass	1 NT	Pass	2 ♡
2 ♠	3 ♡	Pass	Pass
Pass			

When West leads the ♠K, declarer is faced with five potential losers. These include one spade, two hearts and two clubs. The immediate concern is the trump suit.

An extremely old chestnut is for declarer to win the spade

and to return the suit. If West can be conned into leading trumps, it will be much easier to hold the trump losers to one than if declarer has to play trumps himself. The reason this should not work is that nowadays, the art of signals has advanced enough that East can show West how many spades he has.

A much better falsecard by South is to duck the first spade entirely. West will know declarer has the ♠A, but he won't be at all sure of how many.

Perhaps West should not lead trump anyway, but declarer's spade duck may make the trump switch attractive.

How should you play the trump suit if you fear a ruff?

6

K Q J 10 9 8

Should you lead the eight or the nine for example?

Both vulnerable — West deals

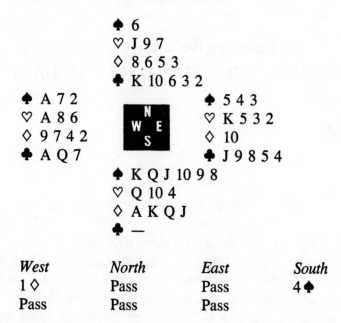

```
            ♠ 6
            ♡ J 9 7
            ◊ 8 6 5 3
            ♣ K 10 6 3 2
♠ A 7 2                      ♠ 5 4 3
♡ A 8 6         N           ♡ K 5 3 2
◊ 9 7 4 2     W   E         ◊ 10
♣ A Q 7         S           ♣ J 9 8 5 4
            ♠ K Q J 10 9 8
            ♡ Q 10 4
            ◊ A K Q J
            ♣ —
```

West	North	East	South
1 ◊	Pass	Pass	4 ♠
Pass	Pass	Pass	

South's 4 ♠ bid was a practical effort once West opened the bidding.

West led the ◊ 2 won by South's ace.

Recognizing the danger of a diamond ruff declarer had to find a sequence of spade plays such that West would duck twice.

South started by leading the queen, and when West ducked this, South continued with the nine.

West did duck both of these fearing the first time that East might have the stiff king and fearing the second time that East might have the doubleton jack.

Not good defense, but certainly a possible defense.

Note that declarer must start with the queen. Any other card gives the show away.

Chapter 10

FALSECARDS BY DECLARER
DURING THE MIDDLE OF THE HAND

Crashing

```
          8 6 4

          A K 7 5 3
```

How do you play this suit for four winners?

Basically, it appears that you require a 3-2 split which will occur around 68% of the time. If this suit divides 4-1 or 5-0, then your expectation will be three or even two tricks.

An excellent rule for most bridge problems is to make allowances for misfortune. Sometimes you can make legitimate compensation for bad luck.

Sometimes, even when there is no real way to negotiate certain dangers, it may be possible to enlist the opponents' help.

A common technique is called "CRASHING." The idea is to persuade your opponents to play their high cards when they shouldn't, thus "CRASHING" them.

```
          8 6 4
   Q                    J 10 9 2
          A K 7 5 3
```

In this setup, the suit does divide 4-1 so your theoretical maximum is three tricks.

But, at no cost to South, he can start the suit by leading dummy's eight. If East ducks, the defense will get their two tricks, but if East covers, the defense will get only one trick.

This is known as something for nothing. It costs nothing to lead the eight. But it may gain.

Would you cover if sitting East?

Both vulnerable — West deals

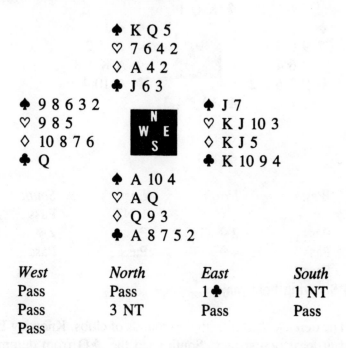

```
              ♠ K Q 5
              ♡ 7 6 4 2
              ◇ A 4 2
              ♣ J 6 3
♠ 9 8 6 3 2                      ♠ J 7
♡ 9 8 5          N              ♡ K J 10 3
◇ 10 8 7 6    W     E            ◇ K J 5
♣ Q             S              ♣ K 10 9 4
              ♠ A 10 4
              ♡ A Q
              ◇ Q 9 3
              ♣ A 8 7 5 2
```

West	North	East	South
Pass	Pass	1 ♣	1 NT
Pass	3 NT	Pass	Pass
Pass			

When West leads a spade, declarer can see only eight tricks, assuming East has both red kings. Some club tricks are necessary.

The best way to get them is to lead the jack. This gains technically if West has a stiff nine or stiff ten. And it gains if West has a stiff queen or a stiff king and East covers.

The second possibility is what actually occurred.

Another spectacular and surprisingly common CRASH is this one.

East - West vulnerable - East deals

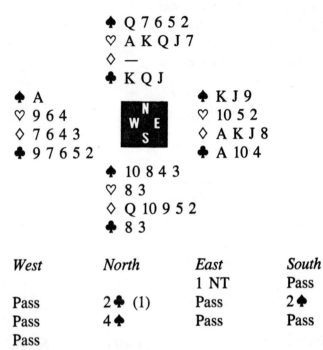

```
                    ♠ Q 7 6 5 2
                    ♡ A K Q J 7
                    ◊ —
                    ♣ K Q J
♠ A                                    ♠ K J 9
♡ 9 6 4              N                 ♡ 10 5 2
◊ 7 6 4 3        W       E             ◊ A K J 8
♣ 9 7 6 5 2          S                 ♣ A 10 4
                    ♠ 10 8 4 3
                    ♡ 8 3
                    ◊ Q 10 9 5 2
                    ♣ 8 3
```

West	North	East	South
		1 NT	Pass
Pass	2♣ (1)	Pass	2♠
Pass	4♠	Pass	Pass
Pass			

(1) Showing both majors.

The defense started with two rounds of clubs. Knowing East had at least two spades, South tried the ♠Q from dummy.

East covered and that was that.

In this case, the contract could, and probably should, have gone down.

If West had held the stiff ♠J, the queen would also have been the winning play.

In no case could the queen lose barring East having a stiff ace or king of trump.

The crashing play most often found at the table is this one. You are in 6♣ with this trump suit.

Q 7 6 4 2

J 10 9 5 3

How should you play the trumps? In this situation, you have two possible plays. One is to lead the queen and hope East covers with Ax or Kx.

The second play is to lead toward the queen, hoping West will hop with Ax or Kx.

What the best play is depends on two separate factors.

1. If you can tell for sure who has the doubleton, then you have to play so as to give that hand the first play.
    If you know East has two, lead the queen.
    If you know West has two, lead toward the queen.
2. You won't often be able to tell who has the doubleton and in this case, you must fall back on scheme two. This requires that you estimate the respective strengths of your opponents. If one of them is known to be weaker than the other, then choose the play which makes the weaker player play first.

For whatever it's worth, if rules one and two don't give me a clue, I lead the queen. Note that everything said above also applies to trump suits like

Q x x x

J 10 9 x x

You have less chance of a swindle, but it can't hurt to try. Whatever you do, don't start the trumps by leading low from the dummy. That gives the opponents no chance to goof.

If your honor cards are the same, but located differently, you may not have the same options.

8 7 4 2

Q J 10 9 6 3

No one is going to cover the eight if you lead it from dummy. It's not tempting enough. With this combination, you can do little more than lead the queen or jack.

It's true that West with Kx ought not to fall for it but if he has Ax, he may think you are trying to sneak one round of trumps by him.

This is the kind of thing which might happen.

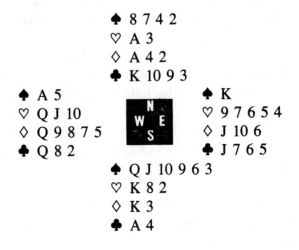

♠ 8 7 4 2
♡ A 3
◇ A 4 2
♣ K 10 9 3

♠ A 5
♡ Q J 10
◇ Q 9 8 7 5
♣ Q 8 2

♠ K
♡ 9 7 6 5 4
◇ J 10 6
♣ J 7 6 5

♠ Q J 10 9 6 3
♡ K 8 2
◇ K 3
♣ A 4

South is in 6♠ against the lead of the ♡Q.

If declarer ruffs a heart in dummy and then ruffs a diamond in his hand, he will have achieved a pseudo strip position. When South leads the ♠Q, West may grab it thinking declarer's hand is

♠ K Q J 9 6
♡ K 8 2
◇ K 3
♣ A 7 4

If this is declarer's hand, West must take the first spade and get out with a spade. If West ducks the spade, West will have to win the second spade and he will be endplayed.

West maybe should not err in this position, but South gets credit for the play.

Not Revealing Your Strength — I

Some of the advantages that an expert has, have come from long hard days or years of experience. It's the way we learn. Few things in this world are easy.

As with most things in life, there are some exceptions and in the world of bridge this is one of them. One of the qualities an expert has is that it is hard to read his hand when you are defending. There always seems to be some uncertainty about what's going on.

If you watch this expert you will note that he gives away very little information for free.

This doesn't means that he keeps a cool demeanor at all times. Hardly, although that would be worthwhile. What it means is that the expert chooses his cards in such a way that the defenders can't draw quick and easy inferences.

For instance:

$$9\ 7\ 6\ 5$$
$$\text{A 3} \qquad\qquad\qquad 2$$
$$\text{K Q J 10 8 4}$$

If declarer leads the four to dummy's five, West will know 100% what the suit is and East will have a pretty good idea.

If, instead, declarer leads the king to West's ace, West and East will both be unsure of the situation.

The squandering of free information comes up over and over. Think back. Has there not been a recent hand where declarer has needlessly given you some helpful information?

```
        ♠ A
        ♡ K 2
        ◊ K J 7 6 3
        ♣ A 6 5 4 2
                        ♠ K 5 4 2
          N             ♡ 8 7 4 3
        W   E           ◊ A Q 5
          S             ♣ 9 3
```

North	*South*
1 ◊	1 ♠
2 ♣	3 ♠
3 NT	.4 ♠
Pass	

West leads the ♡Q. Declarer wins the king, plays to his ace, and ruffs a heart with the ace. Your partner has followed with the queen, nine and ten, which means he has QJ109 and declarer A65. Declarer comes to his hand with the ♣J and leads the ♠7, which you duck. Declarer continues with the ♠8 to your king. West has followed to both spades with the three and six.

What do you do now?

Declarer has six spades, three hearts and at least three clubs. Therefore, only one diamond. You should cash the ace and take the trick you have coming before it goes away on dummy's clubs.

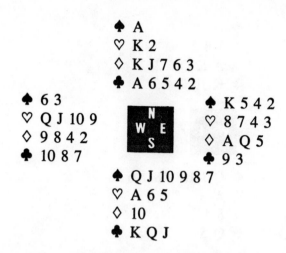

```
              ♠ A
              ♡ K 2
              ◇ K J 7 6 3
              ♣ A 6 5 4 2
♠ 6 3                           ♠ K 5 4 2
♡ Q J 10 9      N               ♡ 8 7 4 3
◇ 9 8 4 2     W   E             ◇ A Q 5
♣ 10 8 7        S               ♣ 9 3
              ♠ Q J 10 9 8 7
              ♡ A 6 5
              ◇ 10
              ♣ K Q J
```

It was not hard to work this out.

What would have happened if declarer had been less free with information. What if he had come to his hand with the ♣K rather than the jack? East might suspect declarer had the KQJ, but he couldn't be absolutely sure. Room for doubt.

And therefore, room for error.

To a lesser extent, declarer gave away his spade holding too, but the bidding had already done that so the defense didn't get much new news there.

♠ —
♡ J 8 2
◇ A K Q J 2
♣ K 10 7 4 2

```
    N
  W   E
    S
```

♠ Q J 10 9 8 7 6
♡ A
◇ 8 4 3
♣ Q 5

West	North	East	South
	1 ◇	4 ♡	4 ♠
Pass	Pass	Pass	

On this sequence, South's spades are a bit of a mystery. South was under serious pressure and might have been forced to bid on a much worse suit.

When declarer wins the heart lead, he should play the ♠Q rather than the six. The queen will leave both defenders wondering about your length in spades. If you lead the six, they will find out quickly how many you have and exactly what the high cards are.

> **RULE — Barring a clear reason to do otherwise, declarer should tend to play the highest of equal cards when he is playing from his hand.**

There are dozens of examples that can show these wrong plays. Remember that you may have a valid reason for playing as described, but in general, you are giving away too much free information.

A 9 2
★

K Q J 10 8
♣

This will help East count both your high cards and your shape.

8 6 2
★

A Q J 10
♣

Whether or not West can win this, East learns about your high cards.

4 3 2
★

K Q J 7
♣

Likewise.

K J 8 5
♣

Q 10 9 7 6 2
★

Awful!

K 4 2
★

Q J 3
♣

Why tell the opponents you have the queen?

I see a lot of these combinations where declarer takes two tricks rather than one to give the show away.

K 4 3 2

A Q J 10 5

The five to the king followed by the two to the ten gives the suit away.

Q 5 2

K J 10 9 3

The three to the queen followed by the two to the nine is another giveaway.

Many of these combinations can be played so as to mislead your opponents.

—

A 4 2   6 5 3

K Q J 10 9 8 7

If you lead the seven, both opponents will learn the quality and length of this suit.

If you lead the king, losing to the ace, and later play the queen and jack, either opponent may hope or suspect his partner has the ten.

K 6 4 2

A Q J 10 9

Play the ace and lead the jack to the king. Either opponent may think his partner has the queen.

Q 9 7 2

5 4   A

K J 10 8 6 3

Lead the ten to the queen. If it loses to the ace, as it does here, lay down your king when you next play the suit. East may think West has the jack.

K 4 2

A J 9 3   7

Q 10 8 6 5

When you lead the five to the king and return the four, East shows out, meaning West has three winners.

Any card you play will not effect your trick count. Play the queen. East may not realize West has the AJ93. Couldn't the suit be like this?

K 4 2

A 8 6 3   7

Q J 10 9 5

Why give the show away?

These various plays won't make that much difference, but once you think of them, you will find them to be almost automatic. Your opponents, as a consequence, will have to work a bit harder and as a result they will make more mistakes than they do now.

Not Revealing Your Strength — II

A family of hands exists where you conceal your strength from the opponents in order to mislead them as to how many tricks you have.

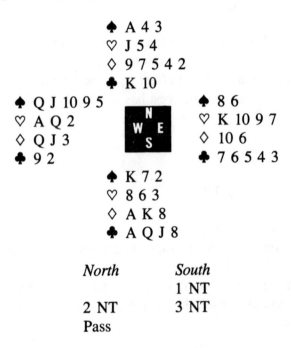

9 7 5 4 2

Q J 3   10 6

A K 8

If you play the ace, king, and eight, the opponents will see you have seven points and three diamonds and that you have four diamond tricks. If your entries permit you might start diamonds by leading the eight or leading to the eight. The opponents may not judge you to have four running tricks and they may misjudge the urgency of the defense.

♠ A 4 3
♡ J 5 4
◇ 9 7 5 4 2
♣ K 10

♠ Q J 10 9 5
♡ A Q 2
◇ Q J 3
♣ 9 2

♠ 8 6
♡ K 10 9 7
◇ 10 6
♣ 7 6 5 4 3

♠ K 7 2
♡ 8 6 3
◇ A K 8
♣ A Q J 8

North	South
	1 NT
2 NT	3 NT
Pass	

West leads the ♠Q won by the ace. East plays the six and South the seven, trying to make the six look like a come-on.

At trick two declarer leads to his ◇8. Should West switch to hearts?

If declarer has played the ◇A, ◇K and ◇8, East would have discarded the ♣3.

Certainly, comparing these two lines of play by declarer, West is more likely to switch to hearts when he see declarer's diamonds and his partner's ♣3.

Variations include these examples:

K 8 6 4 2
♣

A 7 3
★

This is not spectacular but as they say, it's free.

A 6 4 2
♣

K 5 3
★

Why let them know you have the king?

K 8 6 2

J 9   A 10 3

Q 7 5 4

If you lead the four to the king and ace, later lead the five. No one will be sure where the queen is.

A Q 6 2
★

5 4 3
♣

In a slightly different vein, try leading the two toward to three. If nothing good happens, you will take the finesse.

But if East started with Kx, Kxx, or even Kxxx, he may get nervous and take the king too soon.

Combinations like these can be a lot of fun.

```
        K 7 4 2
J 9 3       *       A 10 8 5
        Q 6             *
          *
```

After winning the queen, go back to dummy and lead the four.

```
        K 7 4 2
9 6 3               A 10 8 5
        Q J
```

East will have to guess whether you have Q6 or QJ.

If you did have the QJ, it would be good play to lead twice from dummy because East might duck twice, fearing you actually have Q6.

```
        K 7 4 2
J 9 3       *       A 10 8 5
        Q 6
```

Note that when you lead the two, you are already putting East under pressure. If he goes up with his ace, he gives you two tricks. And if he ducks, he runs the risk of letting you score a stiff queen.

```
        Q 7 5 2
9 6 3       *       A 10 8 5
        K J         ?
```

When you exchange the king and queen, the situation is basically the same.

Stealing a Trick When Time is Lost

Bridge is comprised of many elements. One of them is time. If you bid 3 NT and have eleven tricks, they will do you little good if you haven't time to get them. You'd be just as well off if you had only eight tricks.

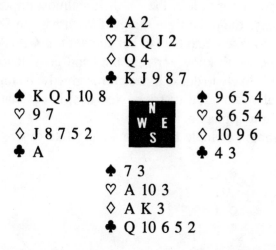

```
              ♠ A 2
              ♡ K Q J 2
              ◇ Q 4
              ♣ K J 9 8 7
♠ K Q J 10 8                    ♠ 9 6 5 4
♡ 9 7              N             ♡ 8 6 5 4
◇ J 8 7 5 2    W     E           ◇ 10 9 6
♣ A               S             ♣ 4 3
              ♠ 7 3
              ♡ A 10 3
              ◇ A K 3
              ♣ Q 10 6 5 2
```

These hands are typical. They can make 6♣ or 6 NT without a spade lead. With a spade lead, you can't even make 3 NT.

When time is against you, it may be fatal. But not always. Sometimes you can steal a trick or two.

```
              ♠ 9 6 2
              ♡ K Q J 7 2
              ◇ J 5 4
              ♣ 7 2
♠ A 10 7 5 3                    ♠ Q 8 4
♡ 8 4              N             ♡ A 9 5
◇ Q 9 3       W     E           ◇ K 10 7 6 2
♣ 9 6 5           S             ♣ 8 3
              ♠ K J
              ♡ 10 6 3
              ◇ A 8
              ♣ A K Q J 10 4
```

West leads the ♠5 to the queen and king.

Cashing six clubs isn't a good idea since it would show East that he shouldn't hold up in hearts.

Better is for declarer to lead the ♡10. It's almost impossible for the defense to do the right thing. If West has the ♡A, he has to guess to take it and then to bang down the ♠A. And if East has it, he won't know for sure the hand goes down if he wins it. East is likely to duck. If declarer is greedy, he might even try to steal a second heart trick. Nervous, but at matchpoints not *too* unreasonable.

Another common swindle looks something like this.

♠ K 5
♡ K J 2
◇ J 10 8 3
♣ K 10 9 2

♠ A J
♡ A Q 7
◇ K Q 7 2
♣ J 5 4 3

North	South
Pass	1 NT
3 NT	Pass

West leads the ♠2 to the five, ten, and jack.

The obvious source of tricks is diamonds. Unfortunately, you won't have enough tricks from diamonds alone.

If you play on diamonds, the defense will win and return a spade, exposing your duplication. You won't have time to get a club trick.

Your best play is to win the spade at trick one and lead the ♣J. If West plays low, play dummy's king. If it wins, you're home. Note that if you let the ♣J run, it would not do you any good even if East won the ace. Not enough tricks.

Here are some combinations where you can try to steal a trick before going about your business.

K 4 2

9 7 3
♣

Risky, but if you need an extra trick early, try to steal the king.

J 4 2

A Q 10 5
♣

If West is known to have the king, lead to the jack.

4 2

A Q J 10
♣

Maybe you can sneak the ten by West.

These plays don't rate to work all that often, but if you are desperate, what else can you do?

Q 10

A 3
♣

I've always wanted to try this. Of course, if it doesn't work, there may be some explaining to do.

J 10 4 2

K 8 7

If you are sure West has the ace and queen, you can lead the seven. Good luck.

When you are weighing the chances of a swindle working, you have to consider how it's going to look to the defenders you're trying to steal from.

Take the earlier example.

Q 10

A 3
*

This looks perfectly absurd, but if you consider it from West's point of view, it looks quite normal, i.e., West will think the suit is something like this.

	Q 10	
K 8 2		J 9 6 5 4
	A 7 3	
	*	

If West ducks smoothly (he hopes), declarer may finesse the ten.

Defense isn't easy and even a good defender might misjudge.

Faking Your Shape

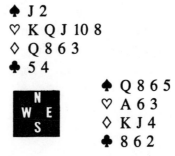

```
        ♠ J 2
        ♡ K Q J 10 8
        ◇ Q 8 6 3
        ♣ 5 4
                    ♠ Q 8 6 5
        N           ♡ A 6 3
     W     E        ◇ K J 4
        S           ♣ 8 6 2
```

South	North
2 NT	3 ♡
3 NT	4 NT
Pass	

Against 4 NT, your partner West leads the ♠ 10 which looks encouraging. You cover dummy's jack and declarer wins with the king.

At trick two, he leads the ♡ 5. West plays the four and dummy the king.

Do you win or duck?

It's usually correct to duck and here there is no substantial clue to do otherwise. You play the three.

The real problem comes at trick three when dummy leads the ♡ Q.

If you could tell how many hearts everyone had, you would be able to duck or grab appropriately. If you could just be sure.

West, in these circumstances, should be trying to help you. His card will be a count card to tell you how many he has in the suit.

If partner has two or four hearts, he will play a high one to show an even number. If he has three or five, he will play his smallest to show an odd number.

In the problem above, the hearts seen so far were these.

```
                  K Q J 10 8
                  *
   4                              A 6 3
   *                              *
                  5
                  ★
```

Putting the above into practice, it becomes clear that on this particular hand, our defensive signals are inadequate.

West's four could be from 42, showing two, or from 974, showing three.

There's no way to tell for sure.

You can guess that declarer would have raised hearts rather than bid 3 NT if he had three hearts. But we all know that such inferences are nebulous at best.

Before looking at the complete hand, try defending this hand with a slightly different bit of information.

K Q J 10 8

4

A 6 3

2

In this setup, it's clear that West can't have a doubleton. The ♡2 and ♡3 confirm this. This means that West has three hearts and therefore, it is correct to take the second heart.

This defense is required exactly.

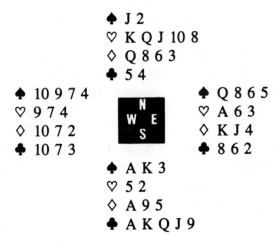

♠ J 2
♡ K Q J 10 8
◊ Q 8 6 3
♣ 5 4

♠ 10 9 7 4   ♠ Q 8 6 5
♡ 9 7 4   ♡ A 6 3
◊ 10 7 2   ◊ K J 4
♣ 10 7 3   ♣ 8 6 2

♠ A K 3
♡ 5 2
◊ A 9 5
♣ A K Q J 9

If East takes the first heart or ducks the second, South will get his ten tricks.

Note what happened here. Declarer had the ♡52. It doesn't seem fair that his choice of plays should make such a big difference, yet it just did.

The reason declarer's play was effective was that he concealed a spot card which was crucial to the defense's signals. An ambiguity was created.

Remember a few pages ago when this suit was discussed.

```
                  Q 8 2
   A K J 7 3               10 9 5
                   6 4
```

West couldn't tell where the four was. If West thought East had it, he would do one thing. If he thought declarer had it, West would do something else.

Much the same applies to defenders' count signals as applies to their attitude or come-on signals.

They can be had!

Not always, but more often than one might suspect.

Here are some examples where a falsecard may help declarer.

```
                K Q 10 8 6
   J 9 4                     A 5 3      ?
                   7 2
```

Does West had J94, J942, or 42? Note that if South leads the two, there is no confusion. Pretty much like the problem hand. One useful observation here.

RULE — The smaller the card that you conceal, the more likely your falsecard will work.

```
                K Q 10 8 6
   J 7 4                     A 3 2
                   9 5
```

East can see all the small cards now so South's deception won't work. South made a nice try but the five was just not small enough to do useful camouflaging.

                    K Q 10 8 4
                        *
J 7 6   A 3 2
    *
                    9 5
                    ★

This time, the missing five does create problems for East. West could have J765, J76 or 65.

                    K Q J 10 9
    A 8 6 4   3
                    7 5 2

Lead the seven or the five, return to hand and lead the other high spot. West won't know if East started with one or two cards.

Some defenders get around this by signaling more enthusiastically when they have four cards, i.e., when holding four, they signal with their top or next to top card.

For example, if a defender wishes to give count, he would do so as in these examples. Note the defender's criteria for these signals. **RULE — Signal with the loudest or most emphatic card available.**

6 2 *	Forced
7 6 2 *	Also forced
7 6 4 2 *	Either the six or seven will be easier for partner to read than the four
J 10 6 2 *	If you can't afford a higher spot, do the best you can
J 8 6 2 *	The eight, if affordable

I actually saw a declarer do this.

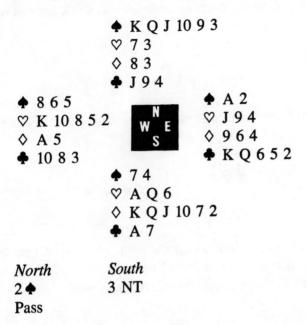

North	South
2 ♠	3 NT
Pass

West led the ♡5 to the jack and queen. Declarer saw that if he could steal a spade trick, he could concede a diamond for nine tricks. Declarer led a cunning ♠4 so that the defenders could be sure he had two spades. East observed he could shut out the spade suit by ducking and he did.

Declarer took no further spade tricks.

But he did make the hand.

Should East have worked it out? Are you sure?

10 4 2

5
★

A 9 7 3

East, at a middle stage of the hand, leads the five.

What should declarer play?

Probably the seven. West will win the trick and whatever else he has to think about, he will think East has the three. This

193

will lead to various misperceptions and ultimately, errors.

Similarly, these trick one techniques will work later as well.

```
              J 8
                       K
              Q 9 6 4 2  ★
```

At a notrump contract, East switches at some point to this suit. Be sure you follow with the six.

```
              J 8
                *
  7 4                     A K 10 5
    *          Q 9 6 3 2     ★
                 *
```

East might read the four as encouraging. You won't be hurting if East decides to continue this suit. You will gain a lot of time and perhaps a couple of tricks as well.

Subtle Leads by Declarer: Overcoming Blocked Suits

One of bridge's more aggravating moments comes when the tricks are there, except for some hidden glitch.

A typical example is a suit which has a built-in blockage.

```
              A K J 6 2
  Q 8 7 3                 5 4
              10 9
```

This is such a suit. If you need five tricks, but have no entry to dummy, you have to take a first round finesse. Further, you can't succeed if West covers the card you lead.

Say you lead the ten and West plays the queen. You have the choice of playing the three top cards, which in this case, will hold you to three tricks. Or you can duck the trick, thus ensuring four tricks against anything but a 5-1 or 6-0 division.

If you need five tricks though, you will require a small miracle.

One way to improve your chances is to lead the nine rather than the ten.

West should cover this, but many a sloppy defender has missed this play.

This theme, plus variations of it, appears frequently, but since quite a few tricks can result from success, it is important to know it.

Here are some examples.

A K J 6 2

10 9

As per the above hand, you should try to sneak the nine through.

A K Q 3

10 9

Again, try the nine. If you have an entry to dummy, you can lead either card (intending to finesse), but if no entry you should lead the nine. The last thing you want is for West to cover.

K 9 5 4 2

A J 10
★

If you lead the jack, West may rise to the occasion. Better to lead the ten.

It's easy to say that West should cover the ten. At the table, it's not always so easy to tell.

```
              ♠ 7 5 2
              ♡ 10 6 2
              ◇ K 9 8 4 2
              ♣ K 5
♠ 10 9 8 3          ♠ 6 4
♡ Q 9          N    ♡ K 8 7 4
◇ Q 5 3     W   E   ◇ 7 6
♣ 10 8 6 3     S    ♣ A Q 9 7 4
              ♠ A K Q J
              ♡ A J 5 3
              ◇ A J 10
              ♣ J 2
```

North	South
North	*South*
Pass	2 NT
3 NT	Pass

West leads the ♠ 10. Declarer wins and plays the ◇ 10.

If West ducks, declarer will get ten fast tricks. If West covers, declarer can either duck it or take it and hope that the ♣ K is an entry.

Both plays run risks.

Conversely:

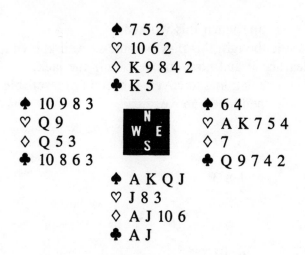

```
                    ♠ 7 5 2
                    ♡ 10 6 2
                    ◇ K 9 8 4 2
                    ♣ K 5
      ♠ 10 9 8 3            ♠ 6 4
      ♡ Q 9                 ♡ A K 7 5 4
      ◇ Q 5 3               ◇ 7
      ♣ 10 8 6 3            ♣ Q 9 7 4 2
                    ♠ A K Q J
                    ♡ J 8 3
                    ◇ A J 10 6
                    ♣ A J
```

Covering the ◇ 10 would be a disaster.

```
                    K 9 5 4 2
      Q 7 3                       J 6
                    A 10 8
                      ★
```

This also would be a poor time to cover the ten.

```
                    K 10 2
      Q 7 4                       A 9 6 5
                    J 8 3
                      ★
```

This swindle works all too often, yet it's hard to judge defensively that West should cover.

```
                    K 10 4


                    A J 9 8 3
                      ★
```

One of the first cons you learned when you took up bridge was that you should start this suit by leading the jack.

If West covers, fine. And if he doesn't, play the king, and finesse East for the queen.

There was a time when this worked.

After a while though, this play became so well known that everyone learned it and now no one covers the jack.

Well, if no one is going to cover, it becomes reasonable to try the swindle mentioned above, i.e.

K 10 2

J 8 3
★

or even

K 10 2

J 8 6 5 3
★

If West misreads the situation, and many Wests will, then declarer will have stolen a trick.

In practice it's extremely difficult to evaluate what declarer is doing and many fine defenders will fall for this one.

Incidentally, when you pull this off against a good defender, he will remember. Then in the future, when you have the real suit, i.e.

K 10 4

A J 9 8 7
★

Your West defender may fall from grace and cover this jack too.

It helps your credibility if you have bid the suit or if you make the play as quickly as possible before the defenders get a count on your hand.

```
              K 9 2
  Q 5 4                       A J 8 7
              10 6 3
```

Declarer can't get a trick out of this if the defenders do all the right things.

Because it's so difficult for the defense to always guess what to do, it's reasonable for declarer to start this suit by leading the ten.

```
              K Q 4 2
  A J 7 5                     8 6
              10 9 3
                 ★
```

West usually ducks in this position and in this case, that's wrong. Declarer can let the nine ride and will end up with three tricks.

West has to cover the nine with the ace or jack to hold South to two tricks. It's a little strange for declarer to play the suit this way, but lack of entries could dictate it. Or, knowledge that West has length could be the reason. In either case, the nine is the play most likely to sneak by the West defender.

Other Subtle Leads

There are quite a few situations where declarer can trade on the defense's inability to tell what's going on.

```
            ♠ Q J 7 6
            ♡ J 2
            ◇ 10 4 2
            ♣ K 7 5 3
```

```
            ♠ A K 10 5 4
            ♡ K 10 5
            ◇ Q J 5
            ♣ A 4
```

Declarer in 4♠ has three top losers and must guess the heart suit correctly if possible.

Declarer's most likely effort will be to draw trump and fuss around with clubs and diamonds. Ultimately, declarer will lead the ♡J.

Clearly on this hand, the last thing East should do is cover. Whether East has the ace or the queen, he has to hold it back.

```
                    ♠ Q J 7 6
                    ♡ J 2
                    ◇ 10 4 2
                    ♣ K Q 5 3
    ♠ 9 3                            ♠ 8 4
    ♡ K 10 9 6         N             ♡ A 8 5 4
    ◇ J 9 7 3        W   E           ◇ Q 8 6
    ♣ 8 7 6           S             ♣ A J 10 9
                    ♠ A K 10 5 2
                    ♡ Q 7 3
                    ◇ A K 5
                    ♣ 4 2
```

West led the ♣8 won by East. Declarer took the club return with the king and drew trump, ending in dummy.

Now he led the ♡J and East found himself involved in a guessing game. Duck or not?

In this case, ducking is wrong. West will win the king, but declarer will later lead toward his queen establishing a discard for dummy's losing diamond.

Similar guessing games can be created.

```
                Q 2
    K 9 5 4                  A 10 7 3
                J 8 6
                  ★
```

West has to guess if declarer has Jxx or Axx.

```
                10 2
    A J 8 3       ★         Q 6 5 4
                K 9 7
```

East has to guess if the actual situation exists and declarer is looking for just one trick, or if declarer has KJx and is hoping to avoid losing two tricks.

```
                    ♠ 8 6 5 2
                    ♡ A Q
                    ◊ Q 3
                    ♣ K 10 8 6 5
    ♠ Q J 9 4                       ♠ 10 7 3
    ♡ J 8 6          N              ♡ K 10 9 7 3 2
    ◊ A 8 6 4 2    W   E            ◊ K 9 5
    ♣ 2              S              ♣ 7
                    ♠ A K
                    ♡ 5 4
                    ◊ J 10 7
                    ♣ A Q J 9 4 3
```

South plays in 5♣ with the ♠Q lead.

Declarer wins, plays a trump to dummy and leads the ♦Q.

Obviously, East should duck so West can win and return a heart.

Would the defense find this play?

Similarly,

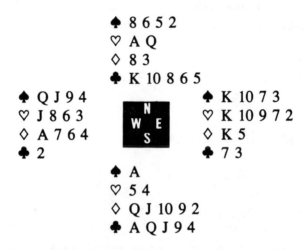

```
              ♠ 8 6 5 2
              ♡ A Q
              ◇ 8 3
              ♣ K 10 8 6 5
  ♠ Q J 9 4                  ♠ K 10 7 3
  ♡ J 8 6 3      N           ♡ K 10 9 7 2
  ◇ A 7 6 4    W   E         ◇ K 5
  ♣ 2            S           ♣ 7 3
              ♠ A
              ♡ 5 4
              ◇ Q J 10 9 2
              ♣ A Q J 9 4
```

Again, South plays in 5♣ with the ♠Q lead.

South's best play is to draw trump and lead the ◇2 toward the eight.

West will have to rise with the ace and shift immediately to a heart.

                    8 3

                  K J 10 9 2

If this were the diamond suit in the previous hand, it would still be a good idea to lead the two toward the eight.

Losing an extra diamond trick is of little consequence if the contract makes.

North - South vulnerable — South deals

```
                    ♠ K 8 5 2
                    ♡ A 9 4 3
                    ◇ 9 6 5
                    ♣ J 9
  ♠ Q J 9                           ♠ 10
  ♡ K Q J              N            ♡ 10 7 5
  ◇ A Q 10 4 2      W     E         ◇ K J 8 7 3
  ♣ 3 2                S            ♣ 7 6 5 4
                    ♠ A 7 6 4 3
                    ♡ 8 6 2
                    ◇ —
                    ♣ A K Q 10 8
```

West	North	East	South
			1♠
2◇	2♠	3◇	4♠
Pass	Pass	5◇	5♠
Pass	Pass	Pass	

After a somewhat stilted auction to 5♠, West leads the ♡K.

This is an unusual hand in that if trumps are 2-2, 7♠ will be cold. But if they are 3-1, 5♠ may be in jeopardy.

Declarer won the ♡A and then cashed the ♠A and ♠K.

With West having three spades, it is necessary that South be able to cash at least three club tricks so as to get rid of dummy's hearts.

If South plays woodenly and leads the ♣AKQ, West will ruff the third round and will cash two more heart tricks.

Better for declarer is to lead the ♣J as if he is considering a finesse. Then, rejecting the "finesse," declarer follows with the ♣A, ♣K and ♣8.

West should perhaps ruff this. But he may not. If South doesn't advertise that the club suit is solid, he may get away with it.

Other variations of this play include these:

A J 10 2

K Q 3

If declarer needs to cash three rounds of this suit before East ruffs in, he can play the king, three to the ace and then the jack. East may think declarer is trying a ruffing finesse and neglect to ruff in.

A Q 9 6 2

K 10 5

If declarer doesn't want East to ruff, he should "finesse" the queen, cash the ace and lead the two. If East thinks South is going to ruff, he may not ruff in himself.

A K 10 8 6

Q J 3

Again, if South doesn't want East to ruff in too soon, South should lead the jack to the ace. Then play the king and six.

You may observe if West gives a count signal in these positions, East should not be confused.

This is true, but you should try these deceptions anyway, for four reasons:

1. East may not be paying attention
2. East-West may not give signals
3. West may misjudge the situation and choose not to give count
4. It can't hurt to try.

Faking Strength or Misrepresenting Your Holding

Almost anytime you can mislead your opponents, you will gain from their confusion.

The way you can mislead and the reasons for doing so are substantial.

```
        ♠ A K Q J 5
        ♡ A J 3
        ◇ Q 4
        ♣ 10 9 7
```

```
        ♠ 10 4
        ♡ K 10 6
        ◇ K J 10 5 2
        ♣ J 8 3
```

North	South
1 ♠	1 NT
2 NT	3 NT
Pass	

West leads the ♡4.

At this moment, you have eight tricks, regardless of your play at trick one. You need a diamond trick and you want to get it without the defense shifting to clubs.

One possible smokescreen you can try is to play the ♡J at trick one. If East covers, you will win, but your exact holding won't be clear to the defenders. They may each hope their partner has your ten spot.

Let's say East covers the jack and you win with the king. You lead the ◇10.

205

If West has the ace, he may not realize you have nine fast tricks and he may hold up. If so, you are home.

If West does not play the ace, you will play dummy's queen. The reason you make this apparently wasteful play is that you don't want East to know you have solid diamonds. You want him to think West has the $\diamond$ J.

Let's say East wins the $\diamond$ A. If he believes either or both of your falsecards, i.e., the $\heartsuit$ J and the $\diamond$ 10, then he may not find the killing club lead.

Now, let's assume the $\heartsuit$ J wins. Is it still correct to lead diamonds?

Against thoughtless defenders, you may get away with setting up the diamond suit. But it shouldn't work.

A better play would be for you to attack the club suit yourself. Lead the $\clubsuit$ 10 at trick two.

One of three things can happen.

1. The defense runs the clubs. This is not what you want and, in practice, it's unlikely to happen.
2. The defense will block the club suit and they will be unable to run it.
3. The defense may be able to run clubs but won't out of fear that you have the missing honors. Some of the time, the defenders will take the club and will attack diamonds. And some of the time, your $\clubsuit$ 10 will win.

For example:

```
               10 9 7
                 *
  A 5 4                      K Q 6 2
    *                           *
               J 8 3
                 *
```

I've see defenders do some strange things. If West thinks South has better clubs, he might let the ten win.

If this does happen, I would probably not lead another club.

206

You can attack some pretty outrageous holdings. In the above hand, you attacked 1097 opposite J83.

When you judge that this tactic is proper, you can "attack" just about any holding.

These combinations have all been attacked at one time or another.

8 2	7 5	K	6 2
J 6 3	Q 4	8 6 4	Q J

The last holding was once played at notrump for two tricks. Declarer led twice toward his hand and was allowed to win each time. He commented that it was a shame he didn't have the ten also, so that he might get another trick.

In 1960, a match between expert teams produced this hand.

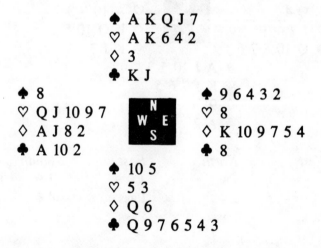

```
                    ♠ A K Q J 7
                    ♡ A K 6 4 2
                    ◇ 3
                    ♣ K J
      ♠ 8                           ♠ 9 6 4 3 2
      ♡ Q J 10 9 7      N           ♡ 8
      ◇ A J 8 2      W     E        ◇ K 10 9 7 5 4
      ♣ A 10 2          S           ♣ 8
                    ♠ 10 5
                    ♡ 5 3
                    ◇ Q 6
                    ♣ Q 9 7 6 5 4 3
```

South arrived in a doubtful 3 NT against the lead of the ♡Q.

The play went, believe it or not, ♡Q to the ace. ◇3 to the queen, which won! ♣6 to the king.

Declarer took his nine tricks.

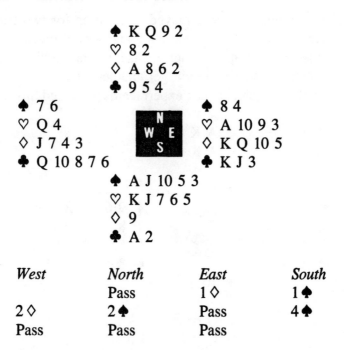

82
★

Q 4
★

A 10 9 3
★

K J 7 6 5
★

This is a side suit in a trump contract. You have guessed correctly to lead to the king.

If entries permit you to reenter dummy to lead the eight, East will almost always go up with the ace which will crash West's queen.

Both vulnerable — North deals.

```
                  ♠ K Q 9 2
                  ♡ 8 2
                  ◊ A 8 6 2
                  ♣ 9 5 4
  ♠ 7 6                        ♠ 8 4
  ♡ Q 4            N           ♡ A 10 9 3
  ◊ J 7 4 3      W   E         ◊ K Q 10 5
  ♣ Q 10 8 7 6     S           ♣ K J 3
                  ♠ A J 10 5 3
                  ♡ K J 7 6 5
                  ◊ 9
                  ♣ A 2
```

West	North	East	South
	Pass	1 ◊	1 ♠
2 ◊	2 ♠	Pass	4 ♠
Pass	Pass	Pass	

West led the ◊ 3 won by the ace. Declarer guessed correctly in hearts by leading to his king.

If declarer continues hearts from his hand, he will ultimately make an overtrick.

If declarer instead goes to dummy with a trump and leads another heart, East will probably take it. This gives declarer time to pitch dummy's clubs on the heart suit making six.

Suits like these can be played deceptively.

Q

A J 6 4 2

In a trump contract, you might play this side suit by leading low to the queen. West might duck, especially if he wants East to get in.

This play could also be correct technically if you feel you haven't sufficient entries to ruff out the suit.

J 2

A Q 6 3

If you feel the king is offside, you can lead to the jack, rather than take a losing finesse.

J

A Q 7 6 3
★

Likewise.

J

A K 10 5 3
★

If declarer knew West had length in this suit and that it would be difficult to ruff three times in dummy, he can try leading the three.

10 4

A K Q 6
★

If declarer needs four tricks from this suit, his best play is to lead the six towards the ten. West, with Jxx or Jxxx may duck.

J 3

A K 4
★

As above, if declarer needs a trick, try leading the four.

♠ 4 2
♡ A J 8 6 2
◊ A 6 5 2
♣ K 3

♠ K 8
♡ 7 4
◊ K Q 7 3
♣ A Q J 10 3

Declarer plays in 3 NT with a small spade lead to East's queen.
  How should South proceed?
  The correct play here is not difficult. In fact, it may not be worth mentioning. But it is worth trying. Run off your five clubs, pitching two diamonds and one spade.
  If a defender does have four diamonds, he may be induced to throw one.
  This play is unspectacular, but is typical of the little things a good declarer does to mislead careless opponents.

East - West vulnerable — South deals.

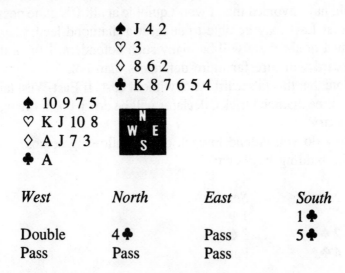

```
                ♠ J 4 2
                ♡ 3
                ◊ 8 6 2
                ♣ K 8 7 6 5 4
      ♠ 10 9 7 5
      ♡ K J 10 8        N
      ◊ A J 7 3      W     E
      ♣ A               S
```

West	North	East	South
			1♣
Double	4♣	Pass	5♣
Pass	Pass	Pass	

You lead the ♡J, won by declarer's queen. Declarer pitches
a spade on the ♡A and leads the ♣J to your ace.
    Your play?

```
                ♠ J 4 2
                ♡ 3
                ◊ 8 6 2
                ♣ K 8 7 6 5 4
    ♠ 10 9 7 5                  ♠ 6 3
    ♡ K J 10 8          N       ♡ 9 7 6 5 4 2
    ◊ A J 7 3        W     E    ◊ K 9 4
    ♣ A                 S       ♣ 10 2
                ♠ A K Q 8
                ♡ A Q
                ◊ Q 10 5
                ♣ Q J 9 3
```

If you didn't cash your two diamond tricks, 5♣ will make.
    Were you taken in by declarer's spade discard? Easy to
understand.

If anyone wants to complain that their signaling methods would have avoided this, I won't quibble at all. It's quite possible that East may be able to suggest a diamond lead.

But I doubt there will be many such defenders. I think the falsecard will lure far more defenders than not.

Note that this falsecard is not without cost. If East-West take their three diamond tricks, declarer will be down one more than necessary.

How do you defend in each of the following setups?
The bidding has been:

North	South
	1 ♠
2 ♠	3 ♠
4 ♠	Pass

In all of these cases, your partner leads the ♠3 won by dummy's queen. At trick two, dummy leads the ♡J. Your play.

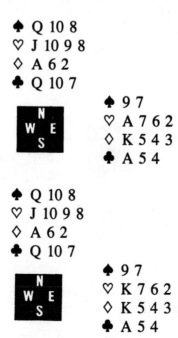

♠ Q 10 8
♡ J 10 9 8
◇ A 6 2
♣ Q 10 7

♠ 9 7
♡ A 7 6 2
◇ K 5 4 3
♣ A 5 4

♠ Q 10 8
♡ J 10 9 8
◇ A 6 2
♣ Q 10 7

♠ 9 7
♡ K 7 6 2
◇ K 5 4 3
♣ A 5 4

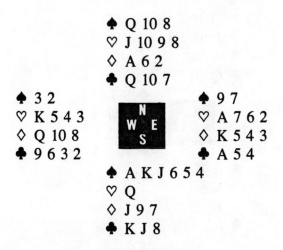

In this setup, East must take the ♡A and switch to a small diamond. A very difficult sequence to find.

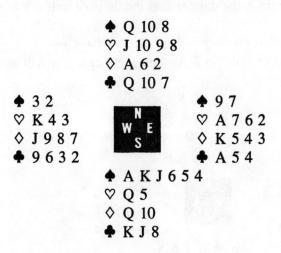

This time, East must duck and West must switch to a diamond.

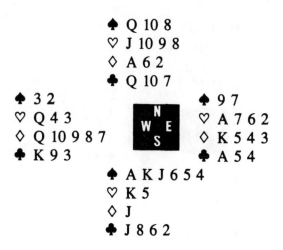

Here you have to duck the heart and hope declarer misguesses.

Note declarer is taking a risk by leading hearts before drawing trump. There is the danger that the defense will get a club ruff.

Perhaps declarer's play is bad. But perhaps not. If it gets a flustered East to grab the ♡A, then declarer's play will work.

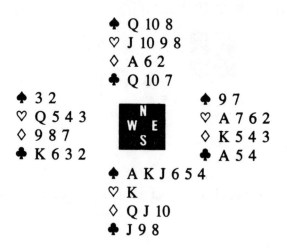

If East ducks, declarer gets his stiff ♡K and his game.

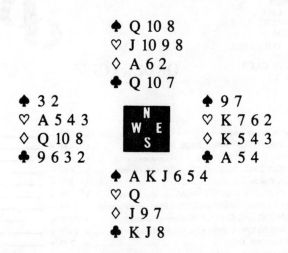

```
                    ♠ Q 10 8
                    ♡ J 10 9 8
                    ◊ A 6 2
                    ♣ Q 10 7
        ♠ 3 2                        ♠ 9 7
        ♡ A 5 4 3         N          ♡ K 7 6 2
        ◊ Q 10 8      W       E      ◊ K 5 4 3
        ♣ 9 6 3 2         S          ♣ A 5 4
                    ♠ A K J 6 5 4
                    ♡ Q
                    ◊ J 9 7
                    ♣ K J 8
```

This is identical to the first of the above hands except that the defense's ♡A and ♡K are switched.

The winning defense is for East to go up with the ♡K and switch to diamonds.

If East ducks, West will win, but this leaves South with a ruffing finesse in hearts. He will be able to set up two heart tricks and will make an overtrick.

What these hands teach is that in bridge, as in life, things are often either unclear, or not as they seem.

Was declarer, in these examples, playing deceptively, or was he making the technically correct play?

The distinction is a delicate one.

DEVYN PRESS
151 Thierman Lane
Louisville, KY 40207
(502) 895-1354

OUTSIDE KY. CALL TOLL FREE
1-800-626-1598
FOR VISA / MASTER CARD
ORDERS ONLY

ORDER FORM

Number Wanted

_____ DO YOU KNOW YOUR PARTNER?, Bernstein-Baron . . . . x $ 1.95 =	_____
_____ COMPLETE BOOK OF OPENING LEADS, Blackwood . . . . x 12.95 =	_____
_____ HAVE I GOT A STORY FOR YOU!, Eber and Freeman . . . . x 7.95 =	_____
_____ THE FLANNERY TWO DIAMOND CONVENTION, Flannery . . . . . x 7.95 =	_____
_____ TABLE TALK, Goodwin . . . . x 5.95 =	_____
_____ THE ART OF LOGICAL BIDDING, Gorski . . . . x 4.95 =	_____
_____ INDIVIDUAL CHAMPIONSHIP BRIDGE SERIES (Please specify) . x .95 =	_____
_____ BRIDGE CONVENTIONS COMPLETE, Kearse (Paperback) . . . . x 17.95 =	_____
_____ BRIDGE CONVENTIONS COMPLETE, Kearse (Hardcover) . . . . x 24.95 =	_____
_____ 101 BRIDGE MAXIMS, Kelsey . . . . x 7.95 =	_____
_____ DYNAMIC DEFENSE, Lawrence . . . . x 9.95 =	_____
_____ PARTNERSHIP UNDERSTANDINGS, Lawrence . . . . x 2.95 =	_____
_____ PLAY BRIDGE WITH MIKE LAWRENCE, Lawrence . . . . x 9.95 =	_____
_____ WINNING BRIDGE INTANGIBLES, Lawrence and Hanson . . . . . . x 2.95 =	_____
_____ TICKETS TO THE DEVIL, Powell . . . . x 5.95 =	_____
_____ PLAY THESE HANDS WITH ME, Reese . . . . x 7.95 =	_____
_____ BRIDGE: THE BIDDER'S GAME, Rosenkranz . . . . x 12.95 =	_____
_____ MODERN IDEAS IN BIDDING, Rosenkranz-Truscott . . . . x 9.95 =	_____
_____ TEST YOUR PLAY AS DECLARER, VOL. 1, Rubens-Lukacs . . . . . . x 5.95 =	_____
_____ TEST YOUR PLAY AS DECLARER, VOL. 2, Rubens-Lukacs . . . . . . x 5.95 =	_____
_____ DEVYN PRESS BOOK OF BRIDGE PUZZLES #1, Sheinwold . . . . . . x 4.95 =	_____
_____ DEVYN PRESS BOOK OF BRIDGE PUZZLES #2, Sheinwold . . . . . . x 4.95 =	_____
_____ DEVYN PRESS BOOK OF BRIDGE PUZZLES, # 3, Sheinwold . . . . . . x 4.95 =	_____
_____ STANDARD PLAYS OF CARD COMBINATIONS FOR CONTRACT	
BRIDGE, Truscott, Gordy and Gordy . . . . x 5.95 =	_____
_____ PARTNERSHIP DEFENSE, Woolsey . . . . x 8.95 =	_____
_____ MATCHPOINTS, Woolsey . . . . x 9.95 =	_____

QUANTITY DISCOUNT ON ABOVE ITEMS: 10% over $25, 20% over $50	We accept checks, money orders and VISA or MASTER CARD. For charge card orders, send your card number and expiration date.	**SUBTOTAL**	
		LESS QUANTITY DISCOUNT	
		TOTAL	

_____ THE CHAMPIONSHIP BRIDGE SERIES	
VOLUME I . . . . x $9.95 (No further discount)	[ ]
_____ THE CHAMPIONSHIP BRIDGE SERIES	
VOLUME II . . . . x 9.95 (No further discount)	[ ]
_____ ALL 24 OF THE CHAMPIONSHIP	
BRIDGE SERIES . . . . x 17.90 (No further discount)	[ ]

ADD $1.00 SHIPPING PER ORDER	**TOTAL FOR BOOKS**	[ ]
	SHIPPING ALLOWANCE	[ ]
	AMOUNT ENCLOSED	[ ]

NAME _____

ADDRESS _____

CITY _____ STATE _____ ZIP _____